Praise for Obstacle Illusions

"*Obstacle Illusions* is a powerful account of Stephen Hopson's life experiences ranging from defeat to triumph. Readers will find themselves laughing and crying and contemplating life in a deep, meaningful way."

Marci Shimoff, #1 *NY Times* bestselling author, *Happy for No Reason* and *Chicken Soup for the Soul*®

"Stephen demonstrates through the power and grace of his personal life experience how nature's support shows up when one is living life with deep inner passion and faith despite the challenges."

Janet Bray Attwood, *NY Times* bestselling co-author of *The Passion Test*

"This enjoyable, insightful book will inspire and motivate you to see opportunities in every problem and become unstoppable in the face of adversity."

Brian Tracy, Author of *No Excuses, The Power of Self-Discipline*

"If you want to be inspired, empowered and entertained, read Stephen Hopson's Obstacle Illusions. His energy, enthusiasm, and can-do spirit is the ultimate prescription for facing life's challenges."

Arielle Ford, creator of everythingyoushouldknow.com and America's #1 book publicist to famous best-selling authors including Jack Canfield, Deepak Chopra, Mark Victor Hansen and others.

"You depend so much on your five senses, but what if one of those senses were taken away from you? Read this book for a captivating look into the life of a man who beat the odds, defied the naysayers, and achieved 'impossible dreams' in a world of complete and total silence."

Sean C. Stephenson, Author of *Get Off Your "BUT": How to End Self-Sabotage and Stand Up for Yourself*

"Stephen Hopson and I met in 1996 in Orlando at the National Speakers Association Convention. He had told me at that time his dream was to learn how to fly. I encouraged him to follow his aviation dreams. He did and succeeded above and beyond what I could imagine for someone who has been deaf since birth. Stephen shows you how to face and overcome adversity in your own personal life and in business. This is a fascinating read no matter what your age or level of experience."

Howard Putnam – Former CEO Southwest Airlines – Speaker – Author of *The Winds of Turbulence*

"Through the power of his own remarkable experience, Stephen Hopson's book, *Obstacle Illusions,* empowers readers to transform their lives by seeing the obstacles they face in a new way. This book is an evolution of mind body and spirit to push readers to see beyond perceived limitations to tap their potential."

Erik Weihenmayer – Blind Adventurer

"Contained within every hardship, failure, obstacle, disability, and mistake is the key to success. You just need to believe you will find it. So even if you happen to be thrown into a river against your will, you'll end up swimming out with a pearl in your hand. Stephen's book is a wonderful illustration of this principle."

Fred Gratzon, author of two books
The Lazy Way to Success: How to Do Nothing and Accomplish Everything
Instant Athlete, Instant Zone: The Discovery of Sports' Holy Grail

"Stephen has a mission: To touch people's hearts and create a ripple effect of goodness around the world. Everyone needs to read this book because everyone needs to tend the heart. *Obstacle Illusions* is heart and soul food. The book, like Stephen, is the real deal; fiercely kind, powerfully peaceful, delightfully determined."

Seth Braun, Bestselling Author of *Indestructible Success,* **Coach and Speaker**

"Stephen's unique experiences in this book as well as his full-throttle optimism and determination are brilliant examples of how to live deeply, fully, and joyfully."

Carol Adrienne, author of *The Purpose of Your Life*

"To a martial artist, every disaster is an opportunity. A tough opponent is your opportunity to test your quality. Stephen Hopson has had his share of disasters, and he's turned them all into opportunities. As I read *Obstacle Illusions*, I alternately choked back tears, laughed out loud and even pumped my hand in triumph. This book is destined to be the next great "feel good movie of the year"! Don't just read this story – *listen.* Listen with all your heart, the way Stephen has to listen. This book is a powerful guide to living life to the fullest no matter what challenges you face!"

Jim Bouchard, Speaker, media personality and author of *Think Like a Black Belt*

"Inside this book are gritty life-lessons from a guy who has a much tougher life than you. Your mission: stop complaining about your life until you've read this."

Mark Joyner, Founder of Simpleology

"In a world stuffed to the brim with hundreds of thousands of self-help, inspirational books, it is refreshing to enjoy Stephen Hopson's unique sense of humor, his unbridled optimism, and his insight that comes from not just intellectual knowledge, but really living what he teaches every single day. I wonder if there's ever a day that Stephen Hopson isn't smiling. If there is, I bet you and I would never see it. Reading his book will add a smile to your day, and if you live by his principles, you'll probably be smiling more than you were before."

Azriela Jaffe, speaker and author of twelve books

Obstacle Illusions

Transforming Adversity into Success

Stephen J. Hopson

Obstacle Illusions

Transforming Adversity into Success

Stephen J. Hopson

© Stephen J. Hopson 2011

Published by 1stWorld Publishing
P.O. Box 2211, Fairfield, Iowa 52556
tel: 641-209-5000 • fax: 866-440-5234
web: www.1stworldpublishing.com

First Edition

LCCN: 2010932663
SoftCover ISBN: 978-1-4218-9162-0
HardCover ISBN: 978-1-4218-9163-7
eBook ISBN: 978-1-4218-9164-4

This material has been written and published solely for educational purposes. The author and the publisher shall have neither liability or responsibility to any person or entity with respect to any loss, damage or injury caused or alleged to be caused directly or indirectly by the information contained in this book.

Best wishes!

Stephen J. Hsu

CONTENTS

Part III: Wall Street

Part IV: Learning to Trust

Part V: The Sky's the Limit!

ACKNOWLEDGMENTS

I began writing shortly after leaving Wall Street in 1998—I practically lived in coffee shops in those days! It was a time of self-discovery, when I learned that I had a talent and passion for writing.

Pretty soon I was formulating short stories and submitting them to various places throughout the Internet like heartwarmers4u and Chicken Soup for the Soul. To my surprise, three different stories I wrote were eventually accepted for publication in best-selling books like *Chicken Soup for the College Soul* (July 1999), *heartwarmers* (April 2000) and *Magical Souvenirs: True Spiritual Adventures from around the World* (March 2002). That gave me more confidence to keep writing.

Two years after I left Wall Street, I had written enough stories to turn them into a book. The first manuscript was created in 2000, and I called upon the help of several people to read through it and provide suggestions. They are: Patrick Combs, Esther Yang, Mark Schall and Sylvia Marie Majewska. Thank you for providing the spark of inspiration to begin the long journey toward the making of this book! You guys are awesome, wherever you are! I told you I would never forget you.

Seven years later, I picked up the manuscript and decided to add more chapters, causing it to grow to more than 300 pages.

That year, 2007, I invited a new group of people to help me review and edit the much larger manuscript. They are: Cari Baker Dubiel, Quint Jensen, Susan Aldrich, Wendy Schwarz, Marc Bernstein, Karen Putz, Les Stoute and Jeanne Dininni. Thanks to many of your suggestions, it was decided to break down the bulging manuscript into two separate books, one of which you are now holding in your hands. The other one will be turned into another book sometime in the future.

I am deeply grateful this book has finally made it to the light for you to read and talk about. I also thank my family. Mom, who spent countless hours teaching me how to speak and fend for myself (Now don't forget to take your pocketbook out of the trunk!). Dad, who showed me what I was truly capable of doing and motivated me to find a way around obstacle illusions (Remember the sign for the word "profit"?). And my siblings, Dawn, Michelle and Matthew, as well as their families, for their love and support.

Maharishi Mahesh Yogi for his life-changing Transcendental Meditation technique, deep profound knowledge and a simple reminder that we need not struggle for the things we want in life because we each have the ability to draw upon the unlimited reservoir of creative intelligence inside us.

My mentor Howard Putnam, former CEO of Southwest Airlines, for believing in my aviation dreams and wholeheartedly supporting me in the quest to take my speaking career to the next level.

My publisher, Rodney Charles, Ed Spinella and everyone at 1st World Publishing, who believed in the potential of this book to impact countless lives.

Bill Corwin, formerly at Bank of New York, for hiring me right out of college in the early 80's when no one would even take a look at my resume.

Andy Williams, formerly at Merrill Lynch, who didn't quite know what to do with me during the grueling interviewing process but ended up hiring me based on a daring statement I made on the last day of the interview. The risk you took paid off in spades, didn't it?

American Winds Flight Academy (Akron, OH) for sponsoring me in my quest to become the world's first deaf instrument rated pilot in 2006. Now that I have the instrument rating, I'll never have another one of those "never again aviation experiences"!

Jennifer Hawthorne for her professional editing skills and helping me polish off the manuscript one final time before publication.

Katie Cleary, Clarity Coach for helping me shape and reshape chapter exercises to make the reading of this book a more rich and interactive experience for the readers.

Leslee Goldstein for proofing one of the earlier manuscripts and commenting on what the title and subtitle should be. You rock!

Donna Cutting and Jim Bouchard for their advice relating to the book publishing industry. Your advice was extremely valuable and made me aware of things I hadn't known about before.

The following people for their take on the early and subsequent book cover designs: Patrick Combs, Amar Sastry, Mary Montgomery, Howard Putnam, Jeannie Dininni, Fred Gratzon, Lawrence Sheaff, Ann Clifford, Miryam Lopez, Karen Putz, Seth Braun, Alexandra Armstrong, Jim Bouchard, Leslee and Bill Goldstein and Carole Mullins. You all know how much I love and honor each and every one of you.

Many word-of-mouth agents who helped promote this book and sell a few copies along the way. I couldn't have done it without your help!

Ken Chawkin for *last minute* proofreading just before going to print—you are an absolute angel for appearing out of the blue and helping me with this!

And of course, Mrs. Arlene Jordan, my fifth grade teacher at Blue Creek Elementary School who inspired the making of this book because of three words she uttered to me in class one day, which turned out to be the tipping point of my life, forever causing a tidal ripple effect that continues to this day.

I am indeed blessed. The whole world is my family!

PREFACE:
TAKE A LITTLE TRIP WITH ME

Come with me on a little trip, if you will. Get comfortable, fold your hands in front of you, and put yourself in a meditative state. Go ahead, do it now.

Imagine for a moment what it would be like to have never in your life heard a sound...any sound. You're completely deaf, and have been since birth. You've never heard a baby's cry, a bird's chirp, an airplane's roar or worse, someone's comforting words in a time of need. You are, in effect, virtually alone in a world of your own.

Now, go deeper into your imagination. If you've never heard a sound, that also means you've never heard a word spoken. Think about that for a moment. If you've never heard a word articulated, how would you know—or more importantly, how would you even learn–how to pronounce a word...any word?

How would you distinguish between similar sounding words in a sentence such as *"The soldier decided to desert his dessert in the desert"*?

Or how about this one: *"They were too close to the door to close it."*

Let's try one more: *"Upon seeing the tear in the painting, I shed a tear."*

Sounds impossible, doesn't it? Do you think a totally deaf person could do it?

Like the person I just described above, I've never in my life heard so much as a grunt, a groan, a roar or a peep. As you might imagine, going through life without hearing is challenging, but by the time you finish reading this book, you will know for sure that obstacles are really illusions, because based on my own experiences, it's not what happens to you that matters but how you deal with it that ultimately determines the outcome. Your life is based on how you perceive yourself and the world around you.

I didn't get to that place of thinking overnight. It took years of self-introspection, taking risks, giving and receiving encouragement and going within for inner strength.

I've encountered every conceivable obstacle you can imagine —obstacles that for the vast majority of people would be considered insurmountable. Yet I've accomplished what everyone else said would be impossible, only because a series of incredible events transpired at just the right time under the right circumstances. You will be reading the highlights of those moments in this book.

The stories in this book represent a natural progression of events that have happened in my life; each ends with a life lesson of some sort—but you may even have your own "ah-ha" moments. Since the majority of the chapters are short, it's conceivable that you can finish this book in one sitting. Through my signature stories, which you're about to read, you will get to experience firsthand how I harnessed the power of risk, courage, faith and hope to get through life's twists and turns (many of these stories are peppered throughout my keynote speeches as well).

Are you ready to roll up your sleeves and get inspired?

Come on in!

OBSTACLE ILLUSIONS

For LISA PLAZA

PART I

THE EARLY YEARS

ONE
NO ILLUSIONS

Mom found out she was pregnant with her first child shortly after she married my dad at the age of twenty-two. Then, a few weeks before I was due, she went into labor in the middle of the night, setting into motion a sequence of events that would turn her life upside down.

From the moment I was born, life-threatening complications set in. One of the nurses spotted web-like veins, then red splotches, all over my tiny body—a sign of severe internal bleeding. One phone call and the hospital was swarming with specialists, each charged with trying to figure out what might be wrong. My mother described the scene as pure chaos.

Eventually the doctors reached a consensus: my bone marrow was not producing enough blood platelets—critical for blood clotting. Both my liver and spleen were found to be abnormally large. They speculated that during the pregnancy, an antibody in my mother's body had destroyed the platelets; without them, I'd bleed to death if ever I cut myself. An emergency blood transfusion was arranged, which undoubtedly saved my life.

My mother was soon released from the hospital, but she walked out without carrying me in her arms because I had to stay behind for further observation. It was months later before I was finally allowed to go home.

I was three years old before it was discovered I had a pair of ears that weren't working. It happened one Saturday morning while I was engrossed in my favorite cartoon, *Bugs Bunny*. Happily rocking back and forth on the living room floor, I hadn't noticed my grandmother, who had come over to give my mother a hand with household errands, entering the room.

As Grandma went about her business, she apparently decided to put me to work (I should have called the Department of Labor to complain) and called out my name a few times. Of course, I didn't respond. Thinking I was ignoring her, she vigorously clapped her hands several times to get my attention. When that didn't work, she called my mom into the room.

Pointing at me, Grandma said, "I think there's something wrong with Stephen. He didn't turn around when I called his name or when I clapped my hands. You try it."

What Grandma didn't know was that my mother was secretly terrified that her worst suspicions about her little boy were about to be confirmed. Because of the nature of my premature birth and ensuing complications, I had been given a series of dangerous chemicals that were concocted and packaged by various drug companies as "medicine." As a toddler I had been frequently afflicted with one thing or another, forcing my mother to shuttle me from specialist to specialist, seeking answers that never came. She couldn't bring herself to ask them point blank whether my brain had sustained some kind of damage.

It didn't help that I wasn't sitting up or crawling at the right time either. But rather than confiding her fears to anyone, she kept them to herself. Occasionally, when the urge was strong enough, she would dance around the issue by asking questions such as, "Doctor, are you SURE nothing else is wrong with him?"

All she could do was secretly hope and pray that whatever it was, it would go away.

Now Mom slowly and quietly made her way across the living room and stood next to her aging mother. Grandma gave her the nod to clap. No response.

"Harder," said Grandma.

I had absolutely no clue what was taking place behind me. I was happily transfixed by Bugs Bunny, probably watching the funny-looking farmer chase after the rabbit with his pointy rifle.

The two of them exchanged glances and knew what the other was thinking: *We have to take him to the hospital first thing tomorrow morning.*

The following day, after hours of testing, the verdict was finally in. Shifting nervously in her seat at the doctor's office, my mother braced for the worst.

"Mrs. Hopson," said the doctor gravely. He paused for special effect before saying, "Your son was born profoundly deaf."

Blowing a huge sigh of relief, she slumped in her chair and began to cry tears of joy. Dabbing her eyes with Kleenex, she whispered, "At least my baby isn't mentally retarded." Nodding in agreement, the doctor allowed himself a faint smile.

Now that the mystery had been solved, my mother could finally do something about it. A week later I was fitted with a rectangular hearing aid box that was harnessed to my shoulders and hung from my neck like an albatross. It created a huge lump on my chest with wires that ran from the box to button-like molds that twisted into both ears.

I absolutely *hated* it.

But I didn't hate what it did for me. Suddenly, a whole new world opened up. I could feel vibrations I hadn't felt before—

and I wanted more of anything that would produce them. Banging together pots and pans in the kitchen became my favorite hobby, much to the chagrin of anyone who happened to be within earshot (which was all the way to the end of the house!). When my poor parents couldn't take it anymore, they'd thump their feet on the floor (to get my attention) and yell in exasperation, "Stephen, stop making those noises!"

After the hearing aids came auditory training—more hardship for my parents. We had to leave home every morning at the crack of dawn to make the 40-minute drive to the hospital, so my Dad could make it to work on time (we only had one car). My mother was forced to spend hours with my rambunctious little sister waiting in the hallway during my therapy, some days feeling as if she would go insane.

In addition, my mother took on the role of teaching me how to speak. It had been decided that I would be taught how to speak and lip-read rather than sign (more about this at the end of this chapter). So while juggling the demands of marriage and two hyperactive kids, my mother somehow made time to get involved with parental support groups, attend medical conferences—and work with me one-on-one with speech therapy.

I loved having Mom all to myself! Dawn (my sister) was usually outside playing with the neighborhood kids, and Dad was still at work, so late afternoons were spent snuggling next to Mom on the living room couch, thumbing through picture booklets.

With the variety of incoming vibrations coming through my hearing aids, I could feel the "sound of my own voice" as well as hers. She'd randomly select a photo or illustration, slide her finger to the corresponding description beneath it, and then place my hand on her throat while I watched and felt her enunciate the word. Once I got a rough idea of how it was pronounced, I'd try to repeat after her with my hand on my throat. We'd go back and forth like this until I got it right. It was painfully slow and challenging. She might try to teach me the word "bear," for example, and all I could say was "baaa," over and over again. You can imagine the frustration for both of us.

Soon it was time for me to start kindergarten. It came down to two choices: Send me to a deaf school hundreds of miles away or try to "mainstream" me in the local school system.

After consulting with an education specialist, my parents decided to start me in a special kindergarten class with other deaf children at a school 45 minutes from home. A year later, they took it a step further and enrolled me in a "regular" first grade class, where I was the only deaf child.

My mother felt she could trust one of the teachers at that school who taught deaf and hard of hearing children, Miss Pauline Winkler, a woman with shocking white hair and kind blue-sapphire eyes who wanted to personally supervise my progress. I remember her as a sweet, warm, affectionate lady who truly cared about me; she always moved her lips carefully so I could understand.

To everyone's delight, the mainstreaming experiment went well.

Just to make sure it wasn't a fluke, the following year they enrolled me in second grade, just down the hall, and continued to observe my performance. At the end of that year, everyone agreed that the mainstreaming experiment was a success and that I was ready to be transferred to the local elementary school closer to home.

I was as close to "normal" as anyone could have hoped.

Food for Thought: We can't control the circumstances we're born into. What we do about it determines the quality of life.

EXERCISE – CHAPTER ONE

Name one or two life situations you were born into where you had no control over. Describe how it feels to have come from that background and whether those feelings have served you well or blocked you from moving forward. For instance, if you were born into poverty or excess wealth (or somewhere in between), have you consciously or unconsciously used that as an excuse to not make some changes with your life?

What has been your general response to the cards that life has dealt you?

Have you used the story of your life to keep you stuck or has it propelled you forward?

Put yourself in a situation you know you won't have any control over like waiting for a bus or going to the supermarket during the busiest of times with long, slow lines. See how you react to circumstances outside your control. If your reaction is negative, take the same situation and re-imagine it with a positive reaction. Feel it, see it, love it!

TWO

THE JORDAN FACTOR

The minute I was placed at the local elementary school, things began to unravel. Not only did I have trouble fitting in, but I also had difficulty telling time, counting money, and reading. Putting me in the front row so that I could lip-read what the teacher was saying was often hampered by the teacher's forgetfulness—they often forgot that I needed them to be facing the classroom, not the blackboard.

Keeping up with classroom discussions became harder and harder. I often relied on the kids sitting close by to tell me who said what, but it got to the point where I did this so frequently that I was eventually met with indifference—a heavy sigh along with a shrug of the shoulders or the rolling of eyes.

Fitting in was so important to me that every time the kids laughed, I laughed along, even though I was clueless as to why they were. Not wanting to look like an idiot, I learned how to adapt and pretended that I knew what was going on around me, especially in the classroom.

Every spare moment was spent trying to keep up with schoolwork. While most of the neighborhood kids finished their homework long before dinnertime, I was often holed up in my room right up until supper, only to return afterward and continue where I had left off.

One night, I was working on a math word problem. For the life of me, I couldn't solve it, so I asked Dad to help out. We had been going over it for more than a half-an-hour and made no progress at all. It was almost suppertime, and the smell of pizza drifted in from the kitchen.

Dad decided to try one last time.

"Stephen, read through the word problem again," he said.

After I had read it aloud, he asked, "Now, do you add or subtract?"

Hesitantly, I replied, *"Add?"*

Pounding his fist on the tiny desk, he yelled, "NO, STEPHEN, YOU HAVE TO SUBTRACT, SUBTRACT, SUBTRACT!" He almost knocked over the green, banker-style lamp. Spittle from his mouth flew everywhere.

The volcanic reaction startled me, causing me to shiver in fear. I wanted to dash under my bed and hide there forever.

Going to school wasn't much better. Kids taunted me every chance they had, calling me names and making fun of my speech impediment and the funny looking hearing aids. When the adults weren't around, they would gleefully plunge the room into total darkness or cover their mouths so I couldn't lip-read what they were saying.

Among the usual cluster of neighborhood kids waiting for the school bus every morning was Patty, a tough little girl with a rather sordid reputation. Twice my size, she pranced around with a "don't mess with me" attitude.

For some reason, one morning she decided to make me the target of her attention at the bus stop. She tried her best to bully

OBSTACLE ILLUSIONS

me by teasing me about something. Rather than fight back, I dashed down the steep hill to my house, wailing at the top of my lungs. It was my first brush with a school bully—who happened to be a girl.

Arriving at the front steps, I pounded the door with all my might, calling out for my mother.

Seconds later she appeared from behind the screen door, wearing an apron and yellow gloves. She was in the middle of cleaning the oven. Her pretty movie star face registered concern in place of her normal sense of calm. I'm sure she feared that her little boy had just gotten hit by a car or something.

Blubbering incoherently, I cried, "Patty's picking on me."

As soon as those words tumbled out, I knew the front door was not opening up anytime soon. I had expected my sorry outburst to convince her to step outside, put her arms around me and sympathetically ask what in the world Patty was doing to her precious little boy. Instead, her eyes quickly narrowed into slits. Slowly folding her arms across her chest, she said in the sternest voice she could muster, "Stephen, you get back up there and go to school, RIGHT NOW!"

"NOOOO," I pleaded. "Come with me and tell Patty to leave me alone!!"

She remained steadfast, firmly pointing up the street and saying, "GO NOW!"

Realizing that she meant business, I spun around and marched angrily back to the bus stop, muttering a string of ugly expletives, thinking, *She's the meanest mother in the world!*

Years later she told me that day was the one of the hardest ones she had ever put herself through. She had desperately wanted to kneel down and put kisses all over her little boy's face and then march right up the hill and give that young lady a verbal reprimand or two. But she knew that if she didn't teach me how to stand on my own two feet, I probably would have ended up as a "Momma's boy." Of course, I was too young to understand that.

Although I was gregarious and appeared happy-go-lucky, I thought of myself as an ugly bucktooth kid with wires that ran from the hearing aid box to my ears, making me look like an alien from outer space. To make matters worse, other parents didn't want me to hang around their kids, because not only did they not want to take extra time to communicate with me (by speaking slowly and clearly for example), they also harbored irrational fears that my disability would rub off on their kids!

No one, especially the teachers, knew what to do with me. I was fast on the way to being held back in fourth grade. But then fate intervened.

Somehow the powers-that-be allowed me to pass, opening the way for my fifth grade teacher, Mrs. Jordan, to make a grand entrance. My mother specifically requested that I have her as my teacher because of her excellent reputation with children.

Little did anyone know that it would be Mrs. Jordan who would forever change my life simply by uttering a short, three-word phrase delivered at just the right time and in the right way.

A larger-than-life woman, with salt-and-pepper hair and twinkling brown eyes, Mrs. Jordan had a voice that boomeranged off the walls of her tiny classroom. She had a powerful smile that made everyone feel really good about themselves.

One sunny afternoon, she asked the class a question. I read her lips from the front-row seat and tentatively raised my hand.

I couldn't believe it—I felt uncharacteristically confident because, for once, I was sure I had the right answer. But when she overlooked the forest of raised hands and called on me, I was suddenly afraid. Here was my opportunity to impress the powerful teacher and show her I was worthy of her love—maybe even show my classmates how smart I really was after all.

I didn't want to blow it. Taking a deep breath, I nervously answered the question.

Her explosive response startled all of us.

Mrs. Jordan enthusiastically slammed her right foot on the floor and whirled her finger a full circle until it pointed directly at me. With sparkling eyes and a wide smile, she cried, "THAT'S RIGHT, STEPHEN!"

It was the first time I had ever gotten anything right. For the first time in my young life, my heart swelled with enormous pride as an ear-to-ear grin spread over my face. I sat a little taller in my chair and puffed out my scrawny chest. My confidence soared through the roof.

It seems like such a small thing—someone simply acknowledging that I had done well. Yet the love and exuberance with which she cried out those three little words signaled a new respect to the other children, and made me believe, at last, that it might just be possible for me to make a place for myself in this world.

Food for Thought: Is there anyone who has made a difference in your life, as Mrs. Jordan, the fifth grade teacher, did in mine? Have you reached out and made a difference in someone *else's* life?

EXERCISE – CHAPTER TWO

Name one or two people who have made a significant impact on your life.

Write in colorful detail how this person reached out to you and why it made such a powerful difference.

Think of a unique way to express heartfelt gratitude toward this person, dead or alive. If the person has passed on, you could create a ceremony in honor of that person or write a thank you note and put it somewhere safe. For those still among the living, if you're still in touch with that person, why not buy dinner for the two of you? If you've lost touch, send a surprise thank you card (handwritten!) or send flowers through 1-800 Flowers. You bet this person will receive the surprise of a lifetime that will cause ripple effects for many years to come!

Now it's your turn – reach out to someone and continue the ripple effect by doing something for someone else. It can be simple as a smile, a few words of comfort, providing a shoulder to cry on or treating a lonely, depressed person to a funny movie. You NEVER KNOW what your actions will have on a person's life. You might even save a life without knowing it!

THREE
ON THE PLAYGROUND

Little did I know just how soon my newfound confidence would be put to the test.

It happened on the playground during lunch recess a week later. It was a beautiful spring day, with sunny skies and a warm caressing breeze that blew across the landscape.

Ten minutes into lunch recess, I saw David, the class bully, sauntering toward me with a cocky swagger, his lips curved into an Elvis Presley sneer. He was the spitting image of "The Fonz" from *Happy Days*, with greasy black hair combed straight back, 1950s style. He always wore a gleaming white T-shirt with a pack of cigarettes rolled up in one, sometimes both, sleeves. Like Fonzie, David did his best to strut his tough-guy image. Up to that point, he had literally beaten up everybody in the whole school, except for me. Not that I was tough or anything, but for some reason he had left me alone—*until that day.*

My body went rigid. *My time has come,* I remember thinking. With steady eyes, I watched him.

The other kids quickly formed a circle around me like a bunch of boxing spectators at Madison Square Garden. They left just enough of an opening for David to make his entrance.

As soon he was in, the circle closed immediately. It was almost as if the other kids didn't want to let either of us escape without first seeing some action.

My heart quickened with each step he took. Nervously licking my lips, I had no idea what I was going to do.

My eyes gradually met his.

Suddenly, as if some unseen force had taken over, I shoved my right palm up, like a traffic cop.

Thrown off guard, David slowed to a crawl.

I licked my lips some more, trying to muster up my courage. Then, my voice dripping with sarcasm, I pointed to my chest and said, *Kid, do you see this hearing aid box?*

The bully snickered and cackled like the cruel witch in *The Wizard of Oz*. His eyes briefly flickered in fear, but no one else saw that except me. It gave me an unexpected boost in confidence.

I raised my voice an octave and screamed, "IF YOU PUNCH THIS BOX, IT'LL BLOW UP THE WHOLE SCHOOL!" My hands clapped like thunder, startling the bully.

His face immediately turned paper-white. His eyes widened and he slowly backed away. As if on cue, the circle magically opened behind him. Then he did something that forever ruined his rough-and-tumble image. The bully ran home as fast as his little legs could carry him!

Folding my skinny arms across my chest, I triumphantly watched the bully grow smaller and smaller. Then I looked around. Some kids were laughing, clapping and whooping, while others vigorously rubbed their eyes in disbelief.

Wow! Did I just defeat the bully?

OBSTACLE ILLUSIONS

Instantly I was transformed into the most popular kid in the whole school. Everyone wanted to be my friend after that!

Sometimes we find out that we do have courage when we're put to the test. The test may not be comfortable, but we become stronger if we face it with courage. Mrs. Jordan's words had given me courage—not just in the classroom but outside it as well. She had made me feel I mattered, and that helped me to stand up for myself. And it felt really good.

Food for Thought: When you know you're important—that you matter—then it's easy to find the courage to stand up for yourself.

EXERCISE – CHAPTER THREE

Everyone comes into your life for a reason. Yes, even bullies from your elementary school days! David and I made a spiritual agreement that one day our paths would cross and we each would have a role to play. Me, the yellow bucktooth kid with monstrous hearing aids and low self-esteem while he played the cocky, overconfident and aggressive kid. Mission accomplished!

Expand your level of awareness and reflect back on your life. Was there any particular person or situation that, at the time, was deemed scary, dramatic, horribly uncomfortable or threatening? Can you see what the lesson was for you?

Write from your own level of intuition and see the light. You may not know all of the reasons why you met this person or experienced that situation. See if you can extract what you learned from the experience.

FOUR
THE POWER OF PERSISTENCE

As a kid I had grand dreams—like becoming a pilot—but I also wanted what lots of normal kids dream of—like a chemistry set, a puppy, a bike and a swimming pool.

And even at a very young age, I knew how to be persistent. My approach with my parents was to prove to them that I was capable of taking care of anything I asked for.

"Mom, if you and Dad buy me a chemistry set, I promise to clean up after each experiment."

"Don't worry about the poop, Dad; if you get me a puppy, I'll go outside everyday and scoop it up."

"Hey, I'll wash and wax my new bike at least once a week!"

"If we get a swimming pool, I'll vacuum it."

Promises, promises, promises! I wonder if Donald Trump was this persistent when he was a kid?

"But you're too young, Stephen," my mother would invariably say in response.

Nevertheless, I refused to stop asking for what I wanted. And despite my mother's reluctance, I could see the wall of resistance gradually wearing down.

For two years I had been asking for a puppy and one day, after I had pressed my case once again, she finally said, "Well, maybe, but I'll have to talk to your father about this." At last, a faint glimmer of hope!

It happened during the summer of 1968. I was eight years old at the time, and my family went on a camping trip to Lake George in upstate New York with another family.

On the third day, my father pulled me aside and said, "Your mother and I have to go somewhere for a few days. You and your sister (Dawn) will be staying here with our friends. They'll bring you back home in a couple of days." He squeezed my shoulders and gave me a bear hug. And then they were gone.

I thought this was kind of odd but didn't pay much attention, because I was having so much fun playing with the other kids. We went for strolls around town and were treated to fabulous lunches of cotton candy, ice cream and gigantic pretzels. We went to the beach and made sand castles for hours. The fact that Mom and Dad had left completely slipped my mind, and I felt sad when we had to pack up and return home at the end of that week.

Arriving home after the one-hour drive, I was retrieving my duffle bag from the trunk of the car when I felt a light tap on my shoulder. It was the mother from the other family.

"Your Dad is calling you out to the backyard; he wants to see you now." Although she was smiling, there was something urgent about her mannerisms.

Puzzled that Dad would want to see me about something so soon, I remember thinking, *He probably has something for me to do already!*

Throwing aside the duffle bag and waving goodbye to my friends, I made my way around the side of the house and headed

OBSTACLE ILLUSIONS

for the backyard. It was enclosed by one of those sturdy silver wire fences. Pushing up the gate lever, I let myself in.

As I tried to close the gate behind me, one of the other kids stopped me. I hadn't realized that our family friends were still there, and apparently, everyone else wanted to come inside too.

What for?

Shrugging my shoulders, I let the gate swing wide open and broke into a trot to where Dad was standing. He was jabbing his pudgy finger at the ground, pointing to a mass of brownish muck. It took me a minute to realize what it was.

"It's poop," my father confirmed. "Go to the tool shed to get a shovel and scoop this up."

"But Dad," I pleaded, "where did this come from? The stupid cats from next door? Why do I have to clean up THEIR MESS?" I was about to throw a temper tantrum.

"Stephen, get the shovel and clean this up now!"

"Ok, ok, ok. FINE."

I felt confused. Dad was being unreasonable. Yet even as he tried to act stern, it looked as if a smile were playing about the corners of his mouth. I didn't understand what was going on, so I stomped off in a huff to the homemade tool shed that Dad had built years earlier, emerging moments later with a shovel twice my size.

I glanced toward the house, where everyone from the other family was watching. Even Mom took a break from her housework to step outside with my little sister in tow, and our next-door neighbors, Bob and Bev, suddenly showed up too. Everybody was covering their mouths, giggling like a bunch of schoolgirls.

I didn't find this one bit funny. Just what in the world was going on?

Behind the fence we had acres and acres of undeveloped land where I often romped around with my best friend, Tommy. That was where Dad told me to toss the muck—over the fence and out of sight. If I threw it back far enough, he told me, it would eventually degenerate and fertilize the ground.

Whoooosh........

Putting the shovel away, Dad then announced that it was time for dinner.

"Stephen, go wash your hands for supper. Use the patio entrance to the house," he instructed.

The crowd of onlookers was still there, trying their hardest to contain themselves while I made my way past them.

Like every kid with enough imagination and smarts, I knew when I had a ready-made audience. Spring-loading myself into position like a high school track star, I ran at blinding speed and leapt over the concrete steps to the elevated patio. Then I turned and waved to my adoring fans.

Just as I started to slide open the patio screen door, a slight movement caught my eye. My head jerked to the left, and what I saw sent shock waves throughout my pint-sized body.

Nestled on a cozy blanket was the cutest potato-sized German Shepherd puppy I had ever seen. She couldn't have been more than a few weeks old. Her jet black and tan body quivered despite the summer heat. Kneeling down, I gently picked her up and cradled her in my arms. Bringing her up to eye level, I carefully examined the puppy and weighed her in my hands, quietly murmuring that I would take very good care of her.

"Your name is Champ!" I suddenly declared.

In response, she licked me all over as if she understood. Her puppy breath made me delirious with excitement.

I turned around to see everyone clapping. Mom and Dad and the neighbors were wiping away tears.

That night I babbled incessantly throughout dinner—no one could understand a word, but I was too giddy to care.

The rest of my childhood flew by with Champ constantly at my side. She was housebroken in record time, and I put her through my own custom-made obedience training program. When I finally did get a bike, Champ galloped alongside like a free-moving spirit. No one loved her more than I.

I know there's a fine line between nagging someone to get what you want, wearing them down until they surrender in exasperation, as opposed to simply asking for what you want. In the case of Champ, I believe that over time, my persistence showed my parents that I was sincere in wanting to take care of an animal, and their risk paid off.

That persistence, based on something deep in my heart, would serve me well later in life. I persisted in my studies at school, even when the going got tough (like learning a new language or writing a tough paper). I hung on through a grueling interview at Merrill Lynch to get the job as a stockbroker. I refused to give up pursuing aviation dreams when everyone told me it would be impossible for a deaf person to be a pilot. I hungrily sought clients while a stockbroker, working longer hours than everybody else.

Everyone faces challenges in life. But persistence is one key that will never let you down.

Food for Thought: The power of persistence goes a long way. And never discount the power of a memorable gift.

EXERCISE – CHAPTER FOUR

We all face challenges in life. Our challenges are one of the greatest divine gifts given to us from the universe in order to evolve to higher states of awareness and bliss.

Jot down instances in your life where you faced roadblocks or challenges where through the power of persistence, you broke through to the other side and manifested your desires.

If you're experiencing challenges right now in your life, what's the one thing you can do that will bring you one step closer to the desired outcome?

FIVE
YOU'RE FIRED!

When I was old enough to get a job during the mid-seventies, I wanted to work at the Sipperly Brothers gas station, just down the street from my house. I told my Dad one day of my intentions.

"Steve, they aren't going to hire you. You're deaf, remember?" I guess he was trying to protect me from the rejection that would surely come on the heels of my job application.

But somehow I mustered up the courage to go for it anyway, completely ignoring his advice. And to everyone's surprise (including my own), I ended up getting hired on the spot!

I couldn't wait to tell everyone the good news. And every night after that, when Dad asked how it was going, I always replied, "GREAT!"

It *was* going great, but one of the things I loved most about the job was drinking coke and playing marbles behind the gas station with Kenny, the owner's son. Unfortunately, Mr. Sipperly didn't agree that this was part of my job description and gave me several warnings to shape up or ship out.

One day he had had enough. Pulling me aside, he folded his

arms, cleared away his oversized mustache so that I could read his lips, and shocked me by saying, "You're FIRED!"

I was goofing off too much, he went on to say. Of course, his son was just as guilty as I was, but in his mind, I was the bad influence around the gas station.

Deeply upset and embarrassed, I hid in the woods for a whole week, pretending to go to work. I didn't want to disappoint my parents, especially Dad, who was so proud of me. How I got away with it, I'll never know, but I knew I couldn't keep up the charade much longer. It was only a matter of time before I'd get caught.

My chance to come clean came one night at the supper table.

"Hey, Steve, how's your job going at Sipperly's?" said the proud father. He was beaming.

Caught off guard, I stopped chewing and gave him a blank stare, suddenly feeling queasy. A thin strand of spaghetti hung unattractively over my lower lip.

Snapping back to reality, I noisily slurped it up, carefully set the fork down, and nervously began rubbing my hands back and forth across my summer shorts.

"Mom and Dad......"

Taking a deep breath, I continued, "Um, I got fired."

"Why, when, how?!?" They were tripping over each other like the characters on *Laurel and Hardy.*

"A-a-a-a week ago. Uh, Kenny and I were caught goofing off a couple of times. Yeah, it's true."

Bracing myself for the inevitable, I sat rigidly and waited for the explosion.

It never came.

Like a cool cat, Dad said, "And where were you all this time when you were supposedly at work?"

"In the woods," I replied sheepishly.

Mom and Dad exchanged amused looks.

My father turned to me and said with a straight face, "Okay, after supper, go to your room and think about what just happened, and don't come out until you've thought about it all the way through."

Relieved that I wasn't getting a verbal lashing, I hurriedly mopped up the last remnants of supper with Mom's homemade bread and made a beeline to my bedroom, where I stayed the rest of the night. I thought a lot about what had happened and became determined not to make the same mistakes again.

Two weeks later, I decided to give myself another shot at getting a job. This time it was a busy pizza parlor at the local shopping mall.

Of course, I told Dad of my intentions, hoping to get his approval. Once again, he tried to discourage me. But I could tell he seemed a little less resistant than before.

That was all I needed.

Encouraged and confident, I went to the pizza parlor and promptly got myself hired. It didn't matter that I was there to clean up instead of actually making the pizza. You never saw a prouder pimply-faced teenaged boy with shiny braces—with a job!

Throughout the rest of my teenage years it seemed I could get just about any job I wanted. I went on to work at other fast food places, got myself a lawn-mowing job at an elderly lady's house one summer, and worked for my aunt, cleaning her place of business.

Over time, I gradually chipped away at Dad's paternal need to protect me. He was learning too. He saw that once I set my mind on achieving something, there wasn't much anyone could do about it. I was going for it, come hell or high water. This mindset would later prepare me for my years on Wall Street.

Ironically, his reluctance to encourage me actually ended up being one of his greatest gifts. While we all need emotional support for our dreams, from another perspective, we can also learn from the people who try to stop us, because they're the ones who help us build character and make us more determined to strengthen our risk-taking muscles.

Clearly, Dad's mission was to play the tough guy. By carrying it out flawlessly, he unwittingly helped me become an award-winning Wall Street stockbroker, transformational speaker, author, and the first deaf pilot in the world to get an instrument rating. Over and over again people told me I couldn't do these things. Yet my father unwittingly sparked fire in my belly by making me want to show him—and the world—that I was indeed capable of doing anything I wanted to.

Food for Thought: Your earliest experiences shape you for the person you eventually become.

EXERCISE – CHAPTER FIVE

Like I mentioned earlier, everything happens for a reason. For me, getting fired was the catalyst to discovering the power of integrity. When I hid the truth of the firing from my parents, it was because I feared the ramifications by telling them the truth. When my father unknowingly fished the truth out of me, all that happened was I was sent to my room to think about my actions. Had I been upfront in the first place, I would have firmly taken responsibility for the situation and owned up to it, which is actually a position of great power.

Are you in a situation where you are keeping information inside you for fear of what might happen? Many of our worries and fears are products of our imagination.

What's the worst thing that could happen if you came clean by admitting whatever it is you want kept behind closed doors? What's the perceived payoff for keeping it a secret?

PART II

FUN AND GAMES

SIX

DARE TAKE RISKS: SWIMMING CHAMPIONSHIPS

From the time I was very young, I was always encouraged to get involved with sports to foster my social and competitive skills. But nothing worked: I was simply not the athletic type. By the time I reached high school, I had tried out for track, baseball, and tennis, but never made the cut. Finally, there was only one thing left: swimming.

My two younger sisters (and eventually my brother) were excellent swimmers, especially Michelle, who won a lot of ribbons in those days. Mom and Dad were always shuttling the entire family to various swim meets, so I got to feel the excitement of competition and witness my siblings' success. It was only natural that I'd want to give swimming a shot.

Starting out on the freshman team, I worked my way up to junior varsity and finally varsity. I improved progressively, eventually specializing in the 200-yard individual medley (butterfly, backstroke, breaststroke and freestyle, in that order). I developed such a passion for swimming that during the summer of 1976, just before my senior year, my parents supported me in going all the way to Fort Lauderdale, Florida for swim camp for some serious training. When I came back a month later, I was virtually unrecognizable—the mixture of sun and chlorine had completely bleached my hair!

As I improved, so did my team, and by my senior year, we advanced all the way to the state championships. I was thrilled when "Rabbit," our coach with front teeth the size of tombstones, decided to enter me for the 200 IM event. And I became consumed with the desire to make the finals.

The day before the state championships, I was watching the 1978 Olympics on television. As I watched the men's freestyle event, a daring idea was born. There was indeed a way to make the finals!

Before I could change my mind, I quickly made my way to my parents' private bathroom and locked the door. The last thing I wanted was to have someone barge in while I was doing the unthinkable. Rustling through the cabinet beneath the sink, I found what I was looking for.

Trembling with excitement, I pulled out a small black case and set it on the counter. It was the electric shaver Mom had used to cut my hair when I was a kid. My heart pounding, I opened the door a crack and poked my head out to see if anyone was around. Seeing no one, I locked the door and got to work.

With the razor whirring to life, I held it beside my face and stared at myself in the mirror.

It's now or never.

Starting on the right side of my head, I mowed in neat lines from front to back, watching clumps of teenage hair tumble to the floor. I was halfway through when I felt the pounding on the door.

My mother!

Stupidly I asked, "Who is it?"

More pounding.

"Okay, okay, just a sec," I said in exasperation.

Slowly opening the door, I positioned my head in such a way that only the unshaved half of my head was visible.

"Yeah, mom, what's up?"

"What are you doing, Stephen?" she said.

"Um, not much, do you need to use the bathroom?" I asked innocently.

"No, *answer my question,* what are you doing in there?"

No sense in hiding anymore. I swung the door wide open.

Stumbling back, she let out a loud gasp, covering her mouth in horror.

Practically screaming she said, "Stephen, what in God's name are you doing?"

"Ma, some of those guys in the Olympics shaved their heads, so I want to do it too. I'm going to make the finals tomorrow," I declared.

Looking up and down at me as if I were crazy, she caught sight of the mess on the floor. It was beginning to resemble my father's favorite barber shop.

With a loud sigh, she pointed her bony finger to the floor and said, "Make sure you clean up this mess!" and walked away, her shiny black hair swinging back and forth like a pendulum.

"Whatever," I mumbled. I hurriedly buzzed off the other half and then lathered my head with shaving cream. A sharp razor neatly cleaned off the last remnants of hair.

Twenty minutes later, I surveyed the results.

Is this what I'll look like when I'm fifty?

It's too late, my boy. There's no turning back!

Since you've already shaved your head, you might as well shave the rest of your body!

Pssssss....more shaving cream.

Sliding in bed later that night, I was in for a rude awakening: the sheets were ice cold! But after tossing and turning for several minutes, I finally fell asleep.

The next morning I awoke at 6 a.m., had breakfast and headed for Albany State University, the site of the championships. So that no one would suspect anything, my head was concealed by a blue bathing cap. I wore nylon stockings and a few layers of T-shirts to weigh myself down during pretrial warm-ups in the pool. The nylon stockings were nothing new: the "hot dogs" (a term given to swimmers who consistently broke records) wore them all the time at practice.

After turning a couple of laps, I climbed out of the pool, dried off, and removed the nylon stockings and T-shirts. The bathing cap stayed in place. Grabbing my blue warm-up suit, I sat in the corner to mentally prepare for the race.

I was very keyed up, filled with tense anticipation about making the finals. This was going to be my day. I would finish in a blaze of glory, showing everyone exactly what I was capable of doing. Closing my eyes, I sequestered myself in the corner, murmured a couple of Hail Mary's and took some deep breaths. A half hour later, I felt a tap on my shoulder. It was one of the "hot dogs" from my team.

"Yo man, it's almost time."

My heart lurched.

Wanting to savor the surprise, I slowly undressed—first the warm-up pants, then the matching windbreaker.

Then, with a dramatic flair, I snatched off the blue bathing cap and tossed it in the air, Mary Tyler Moore style.

The "hot dog" nearly fell into the pool. He let out a guttural scream, "Hey, Hoppy (my high school nickname) shaaaaaved!"

The look on everyone's face was priceless. Rabbit's teeth seemed to stick out even more as he stared at me in shock. It was a comical moment, helping me release a little of the pressure I was feeling.

Smiling, I made my way to the starting block. Everybody gave me high fives on the way over.

Arriving at block # 5, I took one last look at my family up in the spectator section and gave them thumbs up. Snapping the goggles in place, I stepped onto the block, loosening my arms and legs, Olympics-style.

Cocking my head slightly, I waited for the magic words to come from the starter's lips.

Take your mark!

The swimmers instantly spring-loaded themselves into position. I was the only one with my head still turned toward the starter's gun—everybody else was looking down. The only way I knew when the trigger was pulled was by watching for the flash that came seconds before the sound. As long as I didn't hit the water before the crackle of the gun, I would not be disqualified.

Crackle! Pop!

Splashing into the water, my hairless body sliced through the waves effortlessly. The first lap was over in a flash, and then I eased into the backstroke portion.

If you've visited a public swimming pool lately, you'll probably recall seeing arrow-shaped flags floating across both ends. They serve as visual checkpoints for backstroke swimmers, telling them that they are a few strokes away from the end of the pool. Upon reaching that checkpoint, they are supposed to count a pre-determined number of arm strokes before touching the wall and flipping over to the next lap.

When I saw those flags, I counted five arm strokes: 1-2-3-4-5.

That's when disaster struck.

It happened blazingly fast. Apparently I had miscalculated the number of arm strokes and crashed into the wall, almost knocking myself out. The mishap cost me precious seconds.

As soon as I came to, I pushed off the wall, furiously attempting to catch up, and then switched to the breaststroke. You never saw anyone bobbing their head in and out of the water as quickly as I did that day.

I still have a chance. I still have a chance.

Switching from breaststroke to freestyle, I gave the last two laps everything I had, not daring to turn sideways for air. On the final lap, my eyes were riveted on the black touchpad at the end of the lane.

I still have a chance. I still have a chance.

Slamming onto the touchpad, I ripped off the goggles and gasped for air, looking up at the balcony. My whole family was cheering, clapping, and giving me thumbs up. So was the swim team.

My hopes surged. Glancing at the huge digital time board, I couldn't believe it.

Two minutes and five seconds. It was my best performance ever!

Only the first two places would be accepted from each event for the finals. Excitedly, I let my eyes slide over to the column that listed the order of placement. Mine was number three.

Rubbing my eyes, I looked again. My shoulders sank heavily when it hit me that I wasn't imagining things.

Stifling the urge to cry, I dipped my head back in the water—as if that would wipe away invisible tears—and pulled my hairless body out of the pool.

On my way over to the bench, the coach came up to me, cradled his arm around my shoulders and exclaimed, "Congratulations, Stephen! You did your best time ever!"

Trying my hardest not to laugh and cry at the same time, I said, "Yeah, but I didn't make the finals." His toothy mouth puckered in sympathy, and he gave me a reassuring squeeze with a wink thrown in. I never forgot it.

Meanwhile, the rest of my teammates gave me high fives, but I couldn't feel their joy. The back of my head was a throbbing mass of pain. The lump was already the size of a small baseball, and it took weeks to heal.

That was over 30 years ago. Even though I didn't make the finals, it wasn't for lack of trying. Because of my passion for swimming, I was able to take a compelling goal and follow through. As a result, I ended up turning in my best performance, and for that I'm grateful. And I certainly won't be sitting in my rocking chair one day wondering what could have been.

Food for Thought: Do you have a passion for something? Have you considered the possibilities? Why not go for it? Life is short!

EXERCISE – CHAPTER SIX

The universe generously rewards those who take risks and step out of their comfort zone. Many entrepreneurs have gone against prevailing beliefs to bring a product or service to market by taking huge leaps of faith and going for it. Playing safe will never get anyone anywhere.

Is there something in your life you really want to do, be or have but you're always been afraid of losing something in the process? For example, is there someone you're attracted to but you're afraid of rejection? I have friends who are terrified of going up to an attractive person of the opposite sex (as well as the same sex) but can't bring themselves to even say hello. One of them got so fed up with this fear of rejection that he decided to approach every gorgeous woman in a local bar every night for one whole week and just start a conversation. At first he was terrified but the more he did it, the easier it got.

Why not make a decision to approach someone like that just for the heck of it and see what happens?

First write down the thing you want to do that scares the heck out of you. What steps can you take immediately toward that endeavor? THEN GO DO IT.

SEVEN
THE ELEVATOR INCIDENT

In the fall of 1980, I was a junior at Marist College, a private liberal arts school nestled comfortably on the banks of the Hudson River halfway between Albany, New York and New York City. I was studying business administration with a concentration in finance, preparing for my years on Wall Street, which would follow shortly after graduation in 1982. I was known as somewhat of a prankster, but one particular experience stood out.

One day, I stepped into an empty elevator on the ninth floor of my dorm building and repeatedly pressed "G," as if that would make things move faster. I was running late, for I had overslept that morning. When the elevator doors swung open, I stepped inside, relieved that it was empty. I hoped it wouldn't have to stop on the way down. I've never been fond of those times when people squeezed themselves in a tiny elevator like sardines in a can with a row of blank, expressionless eyes staring up at the flashing numbers.

But the elevator had hardly begun its journey to the ground floor when I sensed it slowing down already.

Oh no!

Looking at my watch, I had less than five minutes to make it to class. I grew impatient.

The elevator doors cranked open on the eighth floor and a girl resembling Monica Lewinsky bounced inside. The elevator dipped considerably. "Good morning," she said cheerily. She also pressed "G" repeatedly. Was she in a hurry too?

"Uh, good morning," I replied. My eyes automatically turned upward toward the panel of flashing numbers.

At one point, somewhere between the 6th and 5th floors, I noticed "Monica" becoming somewhat agitated. She was frantically looking around the elevator.

"What's that funny noise?" she said.

I knew exactly what was happening. The noise had nothing to do with the elevator.

Should I reassure her that everything was okay or should I have a little fun with this?

The mischievous little kid in me decided to have fun.

Feigning a look of great concern, I said convincingly, "What's wrong?"

"I'm hearing a weird whistling sound—something's not right with this elevator!" I could tell by her facial expression that her voice rose several octaves.

Gasping in mock horror, I said, "Really, oh yes, MY GOD, I think you're right!"

"Monica" immediately wrapped her arm around mine, holding on for dear life. Practically hyperventilating, she pressed "G" even harder.

When we finally reached the ground floor, "Monica" broke free and lunged forward in an attempt to slide her body through the narrow opening, and then she was gone.

I stood there, dumbfounded. Had I let my little joke go too far? I felt a tidal wave of guilt wash over me. I made a mental note to seek her out and make amends.

An opportunity to do just that came the next day, when I spotted her on a bench under a large weeping willow tree outside the main classroom building, reading a book. I approached her cautiously.

"Hey, there, do you have a sec?" I said hesitantly.

"Sure." Her jet black hair swayed with the wind, partially obscuring her face. With two fingers, she expertly pulled away the last strands of hair and parked them behind both ears.

"Remember yesterday when you heard that funny sound in the elevator?"

"Oh, how could I not! Did you hear it too?"

"Well, um, not exactly. I have a confession to make."

Her eyebrows shot up.

Moistening my lips, I said, "First of all, I'm deaf. Did you know that? And secondly, that noise you heard had nothing to do with the elevator. *It came from me.*"

"What!?? What do you mean?" She uncrossed her legs and set the book aside. I had her full attention.

"Well, it's like this. You see the hearing aid I'm wearing in my right ear?" I turned my head to show her.

She nodded, "Uh-huh..."

"When you stepped in the elevator, I smiled back at you and that caused the noise you heard."

Scratching her head, she cocked her head like a puppy, not quite getting it.

Pointing to the empty space on the bench, I said, "May I?"

She slid over.

Pulling my hearing aid out, I showed her the inside piece, which was made of plastic molding made to exact specifications for my right ear.

"When this molding was first made, it sealed the ear quite nicely. But over time, both the shape of my ear canal and this little piece changed, creating air pockets. When that happens, outside air tends to flow into the ear, causing feedback sounds. The problem is usually made worse when I smile or laugh."

She frowned.

I could see she still wasn't getting it, so I decided to conduct a little hands-on experiment.

"Okay, do me a favor. Smile or laugh, but while you're doing that, put your hand over either ear and tell me what happens."

"My ear moves back every time I smile!" Her face lit up in understanding.

"Exactly!" I said. "If this plastic piece shrinks and the inner ear canal takes on a different shape, that would mean it wouldn't fit as snugly as it once did, right?"

Repeating myself, I continued, "So when the person wearing hearing aids smiles or laughs, it creates a bigger air pocket, because the mold doesn't quite fit like it did before."

"OH, I GET IT NOW." She smiled for the first time.

Then she turned serious for a moment and said, "So you were playing games with me in the elevator?"

"Yes," I said, suddenly feeling uneasy. "I'm sorry. I shouldn't have played with you like that."

Slapping both hands on her thighs, she threw her head back and gave a throaty, Marilyn Monroe laugh.

"So you forgive me?" I asked hopefully.

Wagging her finger at me, she replied, "Yes, but you're one *very naughty boy!*"

Food for Thought: When you're wrong, admit it and make amends.

One of the greatest and most effective tools you'll ever have in your possession is admitting you are wrong about something. Dale Carnegie once said, "If you are wrong, admit it quickly and emphatically." It immediately defuses a potentially explosive situation and gives the other person less ammunition to play with especially if he is trying to "win the game." Both of you feel immediate relief.

Here's something I find myself saying without having to say I'm wrong: "I see what you're saying – in fact, I understand why you would think that." That line has singlehandedly turned around what could have degenerated into a fierce and totally unnecessary argument.

If you're like me, you've engaged in conversations where you felt the need to be right about a point you were making. How did it make you feel when someone else tried to dominate the conversation with all the "logical reasons" why his point was right and you were wrong? In what conversation have you done the same thing?

Write down snippets of conversations you might have had with someone where you admitted you were wrong and describe what happened after you made that statement. Did it diffuse the situation? Were you able to part with a better understanding of each other's viewpoints without having to argue to death over them? How did taking responsibility for your part make you feel? Did you feel better and more empowered?

EIGHT
THE 100 CLUB

One afternoon in November of 1997, I was invited to speak to a group of business executives at The 100 Club in New York City. It was several years after college graduation, and I was just getting started as a public speaker—public because I was not yet being paid to speak.

I was very nervous that afternoon. Arriving early, I wandered around the impressive facility in an effort to calm my nerves.

Since The 100 Club met in a well known private men's club in the middle of Manhattan, their bathrooms were overflowing with shaving cream, razors, combs, mouthwash, aftershave lotions, hair gel, gum, breath spray and everything else you could possibly need. You name it, they had it.

As I straightened my tie and wiped off remaining traces of perspiration, something on the counter caught my attention. It was a strange-looking bottle containing what looked like mouthwash. It beckoned me to try it.

I thought to myself, *Fresh words will pour out of my tingling clean mouth, and I'll speak with power and clarity! Yeah!*

Pouring myself a full cup of the green liquid, I swished it

around in my mouth for several minutes, feeling wonderfully pleased.

Rinse, spit, repeat.

AHHHHHH!

Finally satisfied, I put the cap back on the bottle, threw away the paper cup and took one last look at myself in the mirror. I gave my reflection thumbs up, with a wink for good measure, and headed out to the ballroom.

On the way there, someone walked past me. I tried to say, "How are you, Sir?" but what came out instead was, "OW ARH U, SAR?"

To my horror, my mouth started to feel alien. My tongue swelled to epic proportions and thrashed around wildly, searching for some semblance of normalcy. It felt as if a dentist had injected anesthetic to numb my mouth prior to oral surgery.

Panic stricken, I rushed back to the bathroom and picked up the bottle. The label read:

"The Concentrated Mouthwash is for long-lasting fresh breath. More freshness in a glass bottle for less money!"

I felt ridiculously stupid: *You're not supposed to take on that much of anything in concentrated form!* Of course, my anger only compounded the rising feeling of anxiety. Running out of time, I diluted my mouth the best I could with fresh water and then sped down the hall to the ballroom. Arriving at the door with a wildly pounding heart, I took the deepest breath and slowly entered the room.

The club president was just finishing his speaker introduction.

"......and here is Stephen Hopson."

Stepping onto the stage, I faced the sea of serious-looking

business executives. Beside myself with fear, I could feel that my tongue was still massively swollen. I was afraid to open my mouth and sound like an idiot, but what choice did I have? They were waiting for me to say something!

The opening words were embarrassingly unintelligible, but somehow I managed to explain what happened. The straight-laced crowd burst into laughter—it turned out to be a perfect opener! And fortunately, the swelling quickly subsided and the rest of the speech went smoothly.

The topic?

"Taking Risks."

You can't succeed without having the courage to go on when things aren't exactly falling into place. In fact, as embarrassing as they may be at the time, these experiences often provide great stories for future speeches, books and articles. They become your signature stories, your own unique tales that no one else can duplicate because they happened to you, not others.

Food for Thought: It's not what happens to you that matters but what you do about it that shapes your life in days and years to come.

EXERCISE – CHAPTER EIGHT

Your life becomes infinitely more powerful when you intuitively understand that you have absolutely no control over other people's behaviors, thoughts or statements. What you do have control over is how you behave, think and speak.

Have you ever been angry at someone because your expectations were not met? Perhaps you're friends with someone who is chronically late – never shows up on time. If you are a punctual person, this behavior can be quite bothersome, wouldn't you say?

Many years ago I had a friend who was consistently late, sometimes even up to an hour! It got to the point where I finally decided that I valued my time so after making plans to meet somewhere one day, I said to him, "If you're not there ten minutes after (whatever the time was), I'm not waiting for you." He thought I was joking until he finally arrived 30 minutes after the agreed upon time and discovered, to his surprise, that I was long gone by then. I'm happy to say that he was never late again after that!

This kind of response, that is, changing your own behavior – instead of waiting and complaining – is totally within your power. It sends an incredibly strong message to others that you truly mean business.

Can you think of one or two circumstances that got out of hand and how you reacted to it? How could you have handled it differently? Don't judge yourself for it – just put your awareness on how you will deal with it in a more empowering way the next time the universe presents you with an opportunity to address a similar challenge in the future.

NINE

THE JAMES BOND LADY FIASCO

It took me years to come to terms with my hearing loss. As a kid, not a day went by when I didn't wish I was someone with "normal hearing." It would be a long time before I finally became aware of my inner power and understood that I was on a very special mission to make a difference in the world.

One night I had a brilliant idea. I decided to leave my hearing aids at home and go out on the town for a few drinks. That way no one would know I was deaf—without those hearing aids, I looked completely "normal."

Taking the train downtown to Soho, I entered a trendy nightspot and immediately ordered a martini. I sat at the bar by myself, minding my own business, looking around but not speaking with anyone. Don't ask why I would go out and not want to talk to anyone! But so far, so good.

Just as I ordered a second martini, a lady who looked like she had just stepped out of a James Bond movie walked in. She was wearing a long mink coat that trailed behind her 100 miles, wore a red dress and red fingernails, a red pocketbook and even red shoes. I never saw anyone so color coordinated!

I wondered who she was—perhaps a movie star or something? I gulped down the martini.

Within seconds she slid next to me and proceeded to order herself a glass of red wine, the color of which matched her lips exactly. She was clearly alone, but I did my best to ignore her.

At some point, I ordered a third martini and somehow made the mistake of turning in her direction. The inevitable followed. She said hi. I said hi back. Suddenly we were talking about nothing important. As far as I could tell, my accent-sounding voice never betrayed me. I must have been doing a good job lip-reading because I was responding in all the right places. Every time she laughed, smiled or rolled her eyes, I did exactly the same. She had no clue.

Eventually, we reached a lull in the conversation. I ordered a fourth drink and while I was waiting for it, the James Bond Lady suddenly leaned over and started to whisper in my left ear! Instead of instinctively backing away and telling her that I couldn't hear, I just sat there and acted as if I knew exactly what she was saying. I laughed, smiled and shook my head as if she were the funniest lady in the world.

Suddenly she pulled back and looked at me in a quizzical sort of way. Judging from her look, she was looking for either a "Yes" or a "No."

It took all of two seconds to respond. "Uh-huh, yep, sounds GREAT!" I smiled.

I guess that was all she wanted to hear because her reaction was swift and purposeful. She expertly extinguished her cigarette, gulped down the rest of her drink and dove into the mink coat all at the same time, while barking orders like a drill sergeant, "FOLLOW ME."

As if in a trance, I trotted after her like a clueless Golden Retriever to a waiting cab outside the bar.

While the cab wound its way in and out of traffic on the way uptown, my mind was busy with thoughts, trying to figure out what exactly she whispered in my ear earlier. *We're probably going to a party,* I concluded.

Within twenty minutes, the yellow taxicab pulled up in front of the swanky Ritz Carlton hotel on Fifth Avenue. After she paid the fare, we both breezed through the marble lobby and took the elevator up to the 19th floor. I grew increasingly uncomfortable as the numbers climbed higher on the overhead panel.

Trying to appear nonchalant, I finally asked, "So, where are we going?"

"You'll see."

"Oh."

Arriving at the 19th floor, we stepped out, turned right and walked about halfway down the long corridor, stopping at Room 1960 (I remember that number because that was the year I was born). Pulling out the room key, she turned to me and breathlessly said, "Are you ready?"

Trying to appear like a cool cat, I shrugged my shoulders and managed an unintelligible response, "Nuhhh."

Pushing the card in and out of the slot, she swung the door wide open. My eyes were immediately drawn to the king-sized bed, and what I saw made my knees buckle. I had to hold onto the doorframe for support.

Sprawled across the bed was an assortment of leather chaps, a pair of handcuffs and a whip!

Face paper-white, I slowly turned to her and shakily said, "Hey, listen, um, this really isn't my cup of tea. I thought you invited me to a party or something."

The James Bond lady's face turned into a mass of contorted

fury. Bringing the tip of her red fingernail dangerously close to my face, she yelled angrily, "WHAT, ARE YOU DEAF OR SOMETHING?!?"

"Yesssssss!"

And then I bolted past her to the stairwell, where I practically slid all the way down to the lobby and hopped into a waiting cab—just like in the movies.

When I arrived home fifteen minutes later, I fixed myself a fifth and final martini.

Food for Thought: Be authentic. You were created exactly as you are for a divine purpose. If you don't accept yourself for who you are, how can you expect others to accept you?

EXERCISE – CHAPTER NINE

We've all made decisions that placed ourselves in embarrassing or otherwise dire situations (hopefully not like I did with the "James Bond Lady!"). Despite those decisions, you've actually never, ever made a mistake. This is because everything that happens is nothing more than an *experience*. That's all it really amounts to.

Having said that, have you ever made the decision to deny the very essence of who you are by dressing, speaking or acting in a certain way because you were afraid others would judge, criticize or attack you? Have there been situations in your life where you agreed to do something even if it didn't feel right in your bones because you were worried others would disapprove?

Write down where you could be adding layers of protection to shield you from the reaction of others. What's the perceived reality of withholding this information?

What's the worst thing that could happen if you became more transparent in certain areas of your life?

What's the best thing that could happen?

TEN

BLUFFING AIN'T GONNA GET YOU ANYWHERE!

Sometime during the late eighties, I was at a midnight birthday party in New York City. I could tell the music was at full blast because each of the four strategically-placed stereo speakers appeared to be alive with giant pulsating hearts. The party was just starting to warm up, thanks to a few people who were already herking and jerking their hips like Elaine in that famous episode of the popular TV show *Seinfeld*.

There I was, holding a freshly refilled glass of white wine, surveying the crowd, looking for a place to fit in. Within a few minutes, I spied a group of articulate-looking people chatting incessantly with the birthday boy across the room. They were passing jokes back and forth.

Ahhh...this looks promising, I thought to myself. Taking a deep breath, I promptly made my way over to join them.

To my disappointment, the birthday boy was like that actor from the famous FedEx TV commercial who babbled at 500 miles an hour. I couldn't understand a single word. But not wanting to slink away so soon and possibly draw attention to myself,

I stood there, sipping my cocktail. I nodded, winked and even laughed without a clue. Apparently, the James Bond Lady incident hadn't taught me a thing!

Like a Cheshire cat waiting to pounce on his prey, I was waiting for the birthday boy to say something that remotely resembled a string of words I could respond to. I didn't have to wait long.

"I'm going to buy some condos downtown........"

AH! I CAUGHT THAT!

Springing into action, I brazenly cut him off mid-sentence and practically screamed, "Yeah, I know where to go for that. Have you heard of a cute little shop downtown called 'Condoms Around the World'? Oh, you gotta go check it out!"

What I didn't know was that at the exact moment, for some reason I'll never know, someone turned the stereo all the way down!

At first, a look of surprise registered on everyone's faces. Then as if someone flicked on a switch, the whole place dissolved into a cacophony of hoots, cackles, and wails, with people holding their stomachs for dear life. Some were repeatedly banging on the coffee table as they desperately attempted to catch their breath, while others were giving each other high fives.

Shocked and confused that I could be so profoundly funny with such an innocent comment, but not wanting to be left out, I started laughing too.

My best friend, who happened to be within arm's length, knew better than to think I understood what had just happened. But his reaction was decidedly unhelpful. Instead of grabbing my arm and towing me to the other room where we could talk privately, he waved at me to get my attention and then shouted, "Hey, that wasn't what the birthday boy said. The dude was talking about

OBSTACLE ILLUSIONS

condos, not *condoms!*" More laughter from the crowd. Some friend he was!

I felt as if I were having a hot flash. For the first time in my life, I wished that aliens would magically float down and beam me out of there!

But once again I learned a valuable lesson. I realized that my need to be somebody other than who I was—to constantly try to prove myself—was a sure-fire recipe for disaster. This time, I promised myself that Stephen—just as I was—would be enough from that point forward.

Food for Thought: We all have choices to make. If you choose to bluff your way through life, sooner or later, you're going to get caught!

For the longest time I've bluffed my way through life because I didn't want to ask people to repeat what was being said in a conversation, particularly a group conversation. I hated being the only one who didn't understand what was happening so I'd bluff and laugh along. Needless to say, that made me miserable. One day I had enough and decided that I was going to speak up from now on if I ever got lost in a conversation.

Perhaps you've found yourself in a position of bluffing your way through life in hopes of getting what you want. We've all done that. We think that we're fooling everyone but you can't fool the universe! *Your higher self knows.*

Try this experiment and jot down what happens. Next time you're negotiating for something you want, make a point of being transparent where you *hold nothing back*. Do it even if it makes you feel vulnerable. Put everything on the table. Miracles will unfold right before your very eyes!

PART III

WALL STREET

ELEVEN

HARRY THE ARROGANT BANK BOSS

Every single person who appears on the stage of our lives has something to contribute, regardless of the outcome. They all take on the role of a teacher with a lesson plan for us. For example, David, the elementary school bully you met in Chapter Three, was one central character in my life. If he hadn't approached me on the playground that day, I wouldn't have learned just how much courage I had inside me.

"Harry the Arrogant Bank Boss" was another such character. When I was transferred into his department at a large Wall Street bank in the early nineties, Harry had no choice in the matter: top management had placed me there after I completed two years of financial analysis training in another area of the bank.

It didn't take long to learn that this man had a sordid reputation for chewing out his subordinates over practically anything that went wrong. Harry trusted no one and rarely promoted from within. His inner circle consisted of long-time cronies who were "yes-yes-yes-yes" people. Fear and intimidation often ruled the day and because of that, virtually no one had the guts to challenge him.

Harry was like Jekyll and Hyde. I found myself dreading the

start of each work day because I never knew how it would go. If he was found to be in a foul mood, the staff joked amongst themselves about who would be the "whipping boy" that day (yours truly certainly had his share of that whip). On other days, he'd be in a fantastic mood and babble incessantly about his grandchildren, a favorite topic of his.

At the time, Wall Street was undergoing massive restructuring due to the tremors caused by the 1987 stock market crash. Thousands were being laid off, and job security was no longer guaranteed. You were considered lucky if you had a job. Of course, having Harry for a boss added uncertainty to an already unstable and stressful work environment at the bank.

One day, a friend who had no idea what I was going through was inspired to give me Norman Vincent Peale's classic book, *The Power of Positive Thinking*. It was exactly what I needed. A particularly powerful chapter was called "New Thoughts Can Remake You." Reading that chapter literally sparked a chain of life-transforming events I would never have predicted or been able to orchestrate myself. It introduced to me a timeless and powerful idea: *To change your circumstances, first start thinking differently.*

It took my world by storm. The moment that sentence entered my consciousness, I made a decision that I was going to change my attitude and perceive Harry in an entirely different light from that point on.

So every morning before going to work, I sat comfortably on my black leather couch, closed my eyes and saw Harry as the frightened, insecure human being who ruled the office with an iron fist but who somehow was dramatically transformed into a loving, doting grandfather at home. In my mind's eye, I saw him happily romping around in the backyard with his grandkids.

I visualized this scenario for several months. No one knew about this exercise except God and me. But once this grandfatherly image took root in my subconscious, it transcended the illusion of power he had over me, and I gradually stopped perceiving him as a tyrant. It began to put a positive spin on my outlook at the office.

Although he wasn't aware that I was doing this, he must have noticed the subtle shift of energy taking place within me. Without being consciously aware of it, he began to take more interest in what I was doing, stopping by my cubicle more often just to chat with me. He would ask me questions about the things I was capable of doing, rather than focusing on what I couldn't do. The transformation was startling. No one could believe this was happening.

Over time, Harry began to shift gears and treat me as someone who could be trusted. Rather than keeping me at an arm's length, he seemed to perceive me as an ally, dramatically changing the nature of our boss-employee relationship.

It had gone on like this for about a year when Harry did the unimaginable. On the day of our annual performance reviews, he pulled me into his office and gave me the shock of my life.

"Congratulations, you're being promoted to a senior position!" he exclaimed. He extended his hand in congratulations.

I nearly fell off my chair. Within hours, the entire division had heard about this unprecedented promotion. Everyone thought a miracle had just happened—but I knew differently. What had just happened was completely natural, in accordance with Natural Law; what you sow, you shall reap.

Three months later, an opportunity to work for financial giant Merrill Lynch opened up. It was as if the universe was telling me, "Good job, Stephen, you learned a powerful lesson and now it's time to move on."

Stay tuned for more on that subject!

Food for Thought: People who push our buttons and make our lives challenging are really teachers who are placed on our path to help us grow as spiritual beings having a human experience.

EXERCISE – CHAPTER ELEVEN

We've all encountered people like Harry who knowingly or unknowingly pushed our buttons. Sometimes the encounter is brief, like running into someone on the street. At other times, the connection extends to a period of many weeks, months, or even years.

When we remember there are no accidents, we always learn a lesson of some sort. In the case with the "Arrogant Bank Boss," I learned that love ultimately wins. I also learned how to harness the power of my thoughts: to change my circumstances, I had to think differently.

Are you experiencing less-than-ideal circumstances in your life right now? Try the same visualization experiment I did and see if you can find the good in whatever situation you find yourself. For instance, are you dealing with difficult co-workers or customers? Do you "hate" your job? Do you have a boss you perceive as a tyrant? Take one negative situation in your life and reverse your thinking about it.

Name one or two people, particularly those who might have "rubbed you the wrong way" or seemingly caused you grief and share with yourself what lesson(s) you learned from them. Remember, be gentle with yourself. This is for your eyes only. Don't let your ego judge you. Go within and ask your higher self for the answer and see what comes up.

TWELVE
THE INTERVIEW

Before long, I was itching to make a career change and move on because I knew I was capable of doing much more than working at the bank. Although I had no idea what I would do, I put myself in an open frame of mind and was prepared to seize an opportunity when it came my way. There's a saying that *when you are ready, it will come.*

One day, a friend of mine, a vice president at financial giant Merrill Lynch, told me they were looking for new stockbroker trainees. After telling me about career opportunities there, he asked if I'd be interested in going to work for them as a financial advisor/stockbroker. Realizing I was being presented with an opportunity, I immediately said I would. ("Plan to say yes to opportunities!")

An appointment was set for an interview with the branch manager at the Fifth Avenue location in New York City, where there was an opening. It was a cold, blustery day in February 1992 when I walked into his office.

It resembled a Ritz Carlton penthouse suite, complete with plush carpeting, expensive oil paintings, a king-sized mahogany desk and walls that were covered with sales awards and photos.

His office was a statement of tremendous wealth and success. My cubicle at the bank for ten years was drab in comparison.

The vice president was a young, handsome and successful sales manager who was dressed to the nines. His air of confidence was refreshing. Unlike Harry the Bank Boss, he was articulate and laughed easily. But despite his friendly manner, I was intimidated. The lofty atmosphere was not something I was used to.

We talked for a total of twenty minutes, after which he requested that I make an appointment with twelve of his stockbrokers, all of whom had offices of their own. That meant they were raking in a healthy six or seven figures a year. The vice president also requested that I prepare a marketing proposal on how I would build my clientele if he were to hire me. We shook hands firmly with him wishing me luck.

The more I thought about a new career as a stockbroker, the more passionate I became. Thoughts like "financial freedom," "act as your own boss" and "earn what you put into it" fueled my excitement about a possible change of careers.

I should mention that shortly after my introductory interview, I was struck with a nasty cold, causing me to experience a vicious hacking cough that never seemed to stop. But despite that, I was determined to go through with the interviews; I trusted that life was about to get better.

What followed was an unbelievable series of obstacles during the interviews. Not only was I not feeling well, but every one of the interviewers warned me that the securities business was a very tough place to be. They invariably informed me that 80 percent of newcomers failed within their first year and that there was a lot of rejection to deal with. Some even had the gall to tell me point blank that I was better off playing it safe with my nine-to-five job at the bank!

My stomach tightened with each passing interview, but my

overriding faith more than made up for it. I refused to let their comments derail me. Never before had I been so determined to get my foot in the door!

By the time I went back to the branch manager two months later for the final interview, I was utterly exhausted. By that point, I was starting to recover and the hacking cough was beginning to subside. I walked into his office with my head up high and proudly handed him the 27-page marketing proposal that had taken me days to prepare. To my dismay, he took the proposal and barely skimmed through it before carelessly tossing it aside. The vice president appeared pensive.

He then absentmindedly picked up a paper clip and started to fumble with it, not saying anything for the longest time. The silence was literally deafening. Although the twelve interviews were reported to have gone well, he seemed unsure that I had what it took to be successful.

Suddenly, without warning, similar to what happened that day on the playground, I was seized with an overpowering sense that this was "my moment." My skin felt prickly, a sign that my inner voice was telling me to take action.

It's now or never.

I knew what I had to do, but did I have the courage to do it? My heart hammered like crazy at the thought of what I was about to do.

Pointing a shaky finger at him, I mustered the courage to speak up and say the words that would forever change my destiny:

"Sir, if you don't hire me, you'll never know what I can do for this firm."

Then I did the hardest thing I ever had to do: I became quiet and waited.

The moment I spoke those words, it was as if time crawled to a stop. The vice president slowly looked up at me, stopped fumbling with the paperclip and cracked a smile for the first time since I had walked into his office that morning.

Taking a deep breath, he threw the badly deformed paperclip into the wastepaper basket and said, "Okay, you got the job!"

Enormously relieved, I was halfway out of my chair and was about to shake his hand, but before I could do that, the young vice president dramatically thrust his finger in the air and said, *"On one condition."*

Slowly sinking back into my chair, I half-whispered, *"What's that?"*

"You resign from your job at the bank effective two weeks from today, then come to us and let us train you for three months on a small salary. Then you'll have to take the securities examination. It's 250 questions long," he replied.

Lowering his voice slightly, he warned, "But *Mr. Hopson, if you fail by one point, YOU'RE OUT!"* He made a larger-than-life gesture with his thumb like an umpire calling an OUT at a baseball game.

Although I was reeling in shock at this unexpected turn of events, it took all of five seconds for me to reply.

"Ok, I'll take it." Two weeks later, I said good-bye to an unhappy Harry.

During the following three months of training at Merrill Lynch, I hit the books, acted as a "gofer" for the established brokers, and kept my nose to the grindstone, doing my best.

In April of 1992, it was finally time to take the 250-question securities exam. I took the elevator up to the 4th floor in a beautiful gleaming glass building in downtown Manhattan and followed signs to the testing area.

After showing my ID, I took a seat in the waiting area. From where I was sitting, I could see rows of computers and uncomfortable looking chairs through a window that served as a wall between the reception area and the testing room. There was an assortment of other applicants waiting with me. The whole scene reminded me of an open casting call in Hollywood: they all appeared to be nervous out-of-work actors, biting their fingernails and constantly shifting their feet.

Twenty minutes after I took my seat in the waiting area, the exam proctor led all of us to our assigned computers, gave us appropriate instructions and then told us to begin.

Two and a half hours later, I pressed the enter button on the keyboard. A colorful pop-up window appeared, asking if I was done and whether I wanted to review my answers. No sense in second guessing myself so I clicked "Finish."

A flashing message followed with: *"Please wait while your scores are being tabulated."*

While waiting for the scores, my mind flashed back to the day of the final interview with the vice president, "Mr. Hopson, if you fail by one point, you're OUT!"

I swallowed hard.

After what seemed like hours, another pop-up message flashed on the screen:

"Congratulations, you passed with a score of 83! Please go to the front desk and retrieve a printout of your test results. Thank you and have a good day!"

The national average was somewhere around a barely passing score of 65. From that point on, I never looked back. During my first year as a rookie, I had earned a paltry $16,000; four years later, I was bringing in almost $300,000.

If I hadn't acted on my intuition and boldly told the vice president, *"Sir, if you don't hire me, you'll never know what I can do for this firm,"* I might still be toiling away at the bank, desperately waiting for retirement to arrive.

Food for Thought: When you find your courage, you find out what you're truly capable of doing, garnering handsome rewards in the process.

EXERCISE – CHAPTER TWELVE

It's not the destination that matters but the journey that counts. The journey may be fraught with unknown elements but when you decide you are going to explore your talents and abilities with an open heart and a willingness to take risks, you're bound to discover not only incredible support from nature (giving you all that you'll ever need for the journey) but you'll also garner deep, inner satisfaction that comes with achieving what you (or even others) previously thought wasn't possible.

The universe rewards those who take big leaps of faith. When I quit working at the Bank, I had no idea whether I'd make it. The thought of switching from a salaried nine-to-five position to one based entirely on commissions was a very scary prospect. Even though the end result was unknown, I was willing to listen to my intuition, took the courage to speak up at the right time and never looked back. This experience proved to me that whenever I take risks and move forward with courage, I'll be okay no matter what. The same can happen to you but you have to be willing to set aside your ego, step outside the box and have faith.

What areas of your life are you reluctant to move forward with because you fear the unknown? Do you want to start your own business? You don't have to quit your job cold turkey – you could start on the side and work from there. Do you know you need to get out and network but feel funny meeting new people? How about public speaking – have you always wanted to give a speech but feel terrified in front of a group?

Write down 3 steps you can take immediately to advance toward your dreams. Keep it simple but actionable. Every step you take brings you closer!

THIRTEEN
MISS AMERICA
AND THE SURPRISE CLIENT

A young lady named Heather Whitestone created headlines when she became the first woman with a disability to win the prestigious 1995 Miss America crown. She had become the first deaf woman ever to win the title.

During her reign, she became a tireless supporter of the deaf and hard-of- hearing community. That inspired Merrill Lynch to honor her at a lavish luncheon where the World Trade Center once used to be.

Since I was a part of Merrill Lynch's special deaf and hard-of-hearing investors' division, I was automatically invited to the extravagant affair. I wanted nothing more than to enjoy myself for a few hours, stuff myself with free food and perhaps schmooze with Miss America. When I walked in, I was surprised to see that just about every major media organization was on hand to record the event, including CNN.

As soon as everyone settled at their tables, an announcement was made that Miss America had arrived at the World Trade Center. As if on cue, she waltzed in from the back of the room, wearing a bright red designer dress complete with a large white collar and waving like the Queen of England.

Following in her footsteps were several grim-looking handlers from the Miss America organization. They appeared uptight, probably worried that if anything went wrong, the entire world would know about it in a split-second. Apparently everything, including her grand entrance, was controlled and planned in minute detail.

After a sumptuous feast, the executive vice-president of Merrill Lynch introduced Heather, who spoke to us for about 30 minutes. She concluded her speech by opening the floor for questions.

A quick glance around the room told me that no one wanted to be the first with questions.

Feeling somewhat embarrassed for her, I felt an invisible nudge to do something. I raised my hand like a reluctant schoolboy, not knowing what I was going to ask her. Like my fifth grade teacher did so many years ago, the hugely relieved Miss America quickly called on me.

Not expecting this, I stammered, hemmed and hawed until the most meaningless question came tumbling out.

"How does it feel to be Miss America?" I said, feeling rather ridiculous. I spoke verbally and she read my lips.

I remember thinking, *Why couldn't you have come up with something better than that?*

Well, apparently God had plans for me, that's why.

Unbeknownst to me, the simple act of raising my hand set in motion another chain of events I could never have foreseen or orchestrated.

A week later, Patrick, my sales manager at Merrill Lynch, called me into his office. He was smiling. Slapping his hand on the desk, he said excitedly, "Guess what, Stephen?"

"What?"

"I just got off the phone with the Public Relations department. Apparently CNN wants to come in to interview you tomorrow. Congratulations!"

"Whaaaat? How did they know about me?" I said, shocked.

"I think it was from that Miss America event last week. You were there. Someone from CNN heard you speak or something; I'm not sure."

I later learned that I had attracted the attention of one of the CNN producers. While I was hemming and hawing, he was overheard saying to his assistant, "Who is that guy? We've got to interview him!"

So there I stood, at the door of my manager's office, with grandiose visions of my phone finally ringing off the hook and prospects lining up around the block as a result of my new-found fame. Vigorously rubbing my hands together, I excitedly thought, *Oh Lordy, this is going to be good—really, really good.*

CNN came in the following morning with an entourage that included the cameraman, lighting assistants and the producer. It was exciting and surreal to watch them transform my office into a mini-movie set.

A couple of my clients were invited to appear on camera. While they were being coached by the producer, a make-up artist busily applied make-up to my face. Once the equipment was set, we were ready to roll.

The interview took two hours, which amazed me because the final cut ended up being less than two minutes. Before they left, the producer told me the interview was most likely to get extensive airtime over the following weekend (I've since learned that the media cannot really guarantee when their piece might air because of the possibility of breaking news suddenly taking precedence).

Either CNN executives liked the segment a lot or there wasn't much happening that weekend, because the interview ran continuously, every hour for four days. I thought for sure the entire nation was going to be banging on my door!

But while a few of my friends and family members did catch me on TV, I received one call from a prospect.

JUST ONE.

But what a one it was! A wealthy woman in Seattle had just seen me on CNN and wanted me to be her "investment advisor."

Excited, I labored for weeks, discussing via fax and special telephone calls a broad range of financial issues from investment objectives to establishing a trust fund for her estate. Arrangements were made for her to fly to New York to be wined and dined at an exclusive French restaurant on Madison Avenue—the perfect place to close my biggest deal ever, I was assured by one of the other successful stockbrokers at the firm.

The evening was delightful! The meal was divine, the company charming. She was pleasant and easy to lipread. From my side, nothing was too good for my new client-to-be. Did she want the best wine in the house? Mais oui—it was all on me! Did she want her dish prepared in a special way? The chef said that would be absolutely no problem at all.

That's right, no problem! It didn't matter that the bill would come to a staggering $300, I was going to snag my biggest client ever!

Over the sumptuous meal, we continued to discuss her financial goals and plans. Then it was time for dessert—and the moment for me to close the deal.

As I pulled out some papers from my briefcase, I glanced at her and saw that her face had turned ashen. The smile was gone, and I suddenly felt bile rising from the depths of my stomach. Even before she said a word, I knew that I had been duped. Despite my due diligence, despite all the faxes and phone calls, I really hadn't known her at all. Not only did she not have millions to invest, as she had indicated—she literally had no money!

I was speechless. I was so stunned that I couldn't bring myself to ask why she had flown herself across America on her own dime for dinner with me. It didn't make sense. I angrily threw down my napkin, quickly paid the bill and left the restaurant.

To this day I don't know what happened. Perhaps she had been so impressed by the CNN interview that she wanted to use the potential investor relationship as a way to meet me for something more personal. We never saw each other again.

But once again, God smiled (more like laughed) because He had other plans in store for me.

One day, a package arrived from Merrill Lynch's PR department. Like a kid on Christmas morning, I ripped it open to find two videotapes with my name on them. One was an unedited version of the Miss America luncheon, which was nice, but the second one was what I clearly prized the most. It was a copy of the nationally televised CNN interview, which the producer had thoughtfully sent.

What I didn't know at the time was that it would end up becoming a very useful promotional piece for my future speaking career, which wouldn't happen for another two or three years. I had expected the CNN interview to land me a slew of clients, then my biggest client—but instead it provided me with footage of a national television appearance that would become a cornerstone in my promotional materials for my speaking business.

Isn't it amazing how everything happens at just the right time for the right reasons to prepare you for the future?

Food for Thought: The universe has bigger plans for you, even if things do not turn out the way you think they should.

EXERCISE – CHAPTER THIRTEEN

You probably know that life can be mysterious. Perhaps you've worked hard to advance toward your dreams but somehow life has taken you in a different direction. Have you ever had that happen to you?

There are numerous stories out there of people who thought they needed to head on a certain career path only to be handed a completely unexpected opportunity in an area that they would never before have considered; yet it turned out to be a perfect fit.

Perhaps an opportunity fell into your lap out of nowhere and you were mysteriously led to your divine calling. If that hasn't happened to you, don't fret. You're going to find your life's mission as long as you stay open to the possibilities. I'm now inviting you to open your mind and recognize that divine forces are at work for you. Even though you can't see them, these invisible sources of power are helping you find your way.

Write down snippets of your life where you were so certain things would work out in a certain way yet the end results turned out completely different. It can be anything – big or small. In fact, let me ask you this – do you believe higher forces are at work, assisting you along the way? If so, where have you seen evidence of this in your life?

FOURTEEN
THE GRANDMOTHERLY CLIENT

In 1995, I was finally riding high after a painfully slow start in the securities business. That was the year I lost 20 pounds, clients saw double-digit growths in their portfolios, and I was earning a handsome six-figure income. On top of that, I had won sales trips to exotic places in Mexico and Bermuda, was interviewed on national television (CNN), and accumulated one sales award after the other. It easily passed for my best year to date physically, emotionally, financially and spiritually.

Little did I know that all hell was about to break loose.

There was a woman whom I had affectionately labeled "the grandmotherly client." She was a rail-thin lady with bushels of snow-white hair, whose kind face was overshadowed by gigantic red framed glasses, reminding me of Sally Jessica Raphael, a popular talk show host at the time. Like many of my clients, she was quite fond of me.

We had met at a black-tie fundraising affair one evening in downtown Manhattan. Then one day she came to my office and opened an account with me, transferring virtually all of her savings and investments to Merrill Lynch. In the weeks that followed, we worked together diligently to construct a portfolio in accordance with her investment objectives.

All was well until the market took a sharp nosedive in late 1995, causing investors everywhere to panic. Like everyone else, this scared her. Taking great pains to reassure her that this was only a temporary cycle, I thought I was successful in putting her fears to rest. However, I couldn't have been more wrong.

My eyes widened in horror one morning when the legal compliance officer handed me a three-page letter from her. Contained in the letter were pages of harsh-sounding legalese, accusing me of gross incompetence! My mouth immediately went dry, and I felt as if my body would collapse.

Holding the letter with trembling hands, I thought, *How could this have happened!?*

Prior to my being hired at Merrill Lynch, another deaf stockbroker from a competing firm had made a very bad reputation for himself. He had tricked hundreds of unsuspecting clients into making risky investments, causing them to lose all of their savings. Many of them were retirees who should have been in more conservative investments.

So by the time I joined the securities business, I already had my work cut out for me. If I was to make it, I had to work a thousand times harder to earn the trust of potential clients, vowing I would do the right thing and not steer them wrong. Eventually my reputation for integrity became widely known and I began to attract clients from all walks of life.

Until I was handed that letter, I had succeeded in my goal to never have a complaint lodged against me.

The rest of that week flew by in a blur. I walked around in a daze, losing all interest in the stock market. A million debilitating thoughts ran through my head:

You're going to be fired!

Your ass will be hauled to court!

Your career on Wall Street is finished!

In the days that followed, I kept rereading her letter, not believing what she had written. I must have looked like a shell-shocked zombie, for I hardly ate or slept that week.

It wasn't long before I was called to the compliance office to discuss how we were going to handle her letter. Swallowing hard, I knocked on the huge window that served as a wall between the secretary's desk and the office of George, the compliance officer. He was on the phone, but motioned for me to come inside and sit down while he finished up the call.

George was a kind man who was very well respected and widely known for being fair. As he was talking on the phone, he alternated between reassuring smiles and winks, which I found disconcerting. Perhaps it was one of those "calm before the storm" kind of things. But despite his reputation, I feared the worst was about to happen. Hanging up, he uttered a cheerful greeting and smiled again. Did I want coffee or tea?

"No, thanks." I squirmed in my seat. I wanted this to be over with. Either he was going to fire me or I was going to have to quit.

No one was more surprised than I when he calmly folded his hands and proceeded to tell me that the next step was to simply write a memo to his attention, describing how and why her portfolio had been constructed the way it was.

"Hand it in a week from today," he directed.

That was it. No drama, threats or shouting matches. For the first time since receiving her letter, I saw a glimmer of hope on the horizon. I began to believe the universe would do justice for me in this very scary drama that was unfolding.

I went right to work on the memo, handing it in to George a week later. In the end, it was determined that I had constructed her portfolio exactly in accordance with her objectives. Her complaint was subsequently dropped, after which I never heard from her again.

But I never forgot the incident. It shook me to the core. Sometimes even when you do right by other people and do everything in your power to handle things with integrity, it doesn't stop them from blaming you when things outside your (or their) control go wrong, like declining market conditions.

The incident taught me the first of many lessons on how to banish anxiety when in the midst of a major crisis:

First, obtain the facts. That's what I did when putting together the memo. I gathered all pertinent information, creating worksheets to show exactly what happened from the day she opened her account until I received her letter. I found that getting busy, focusing on the task at hand, made it difficult to worry about the future. It helped me stay in the present.

Next, analyze the data. Make sure it's complete and honest.

And finally, make a decision on a course of action to take and stick to it. In my case, I had no choice; I had done my part and now I handed in the memo and simply had to trust that it would work out.

It did.

Was the grandmotherly client actually an angel in disguise who was part of the plan to teach me a lesson? You decide.

Food for Thought: Fear brings on worry. Worry makes you tense and clouds your judgment. Trust that if you did everything with integrity, the universe will do justice for you.

EXERCISE – CHAPTER FOURTEEN

In my experience, even what we humans consider to be horrific experiences have a divine purpose behind them. While my experience with the "Grandmotherly Client" was truly terrifying, in hindsight I can see why she came on to the stage of my life.

She was playing her divine role in teaching me how to handle a crisis brought on by another person. Even though I panicked and had many sleepless nights, once I focused on gathering the facts, I was able to stay present. When you're operating from that space, it's impossible to worry about the future. Once I gathered all the facts and handed in the memo, there was nothing I could do but surrender to the final outcome – that's called letting go.

Has anyone ever accused you of something you did or didn't do? How did you contribute to the situation? How did you handle it? Be careful not to blame yourself or anyone.

Write about your experiences as they happened and after you're done, go within and ask your higher self how you might have handled it differently. Then imagine the situation with your new insights. The purpose of this exercise is not to remain stuck in the past but to help you raise your level of awareness – after all, the first step to personal evolution is awareness. All you're doing is bringing yourself to another level of awareness and seeing things as they really are.

FIFTEEN
THE KIWANIS CLUB SPEECH

Have you ever thrown a flat rock across a pond and watched it generate a series of ripples? That was the impact my fifth grade teacher, Mrs. Jordan, made on my life when she uttered those three words so many years ago: "THAT'S RIGHT, STEPHEN!"

She didn't know the impact she would make on my life that day. And like her, it's possible that you are making an extraordinary difference in the lives of other people without even being aware of it. I had that chance early in my speaking career.

As I was getting my feet wet in public speaking in New York City, where I was still working on Wall Street, I was invited to give a speech at a Kiwanis Club in Brooklyn. Many a fledging speaker has gotten his or her start by "speaking for food" at civic organizations like the Kiwanis or Rotary. While there was no money involved, I got to enjoy a nice, warm meal in exchange for a 20-minute speech. Too, it was an opportunity to build my speaking skills and try out some new material.

This night, I was planning to share one of my favorite stories, first discovered in *Chicken Soup for the Soul*. It was "Who You Are Makes a Difference,"™ by Helice "Sparky" Bridges, and I thought it would make for a great topic because it made me cry every time I read it. My goal was to illustrate the power of making a difference in other people's lives. But little did I know that by speaking that night, I'd do exactly that.

The club held its meetings in an Italian restaurant in eastern Brooklyn, so I took the subway out there, arriving at the restaurant about thirty minutes early. My intention was to meet the person who would be introducing me, get a feel for the layout of the room and do a sound check (with the help of a hearing person, of course).

Throughout the meal, I sat next to the Kiwanis club president, giving me a chance to get to know him more.

"I'm really looking forward to your speech tonight," he said at one point.

They say that public speaking is the #1 fear people have (death is #3!). It isn't easy getting up in front of a room full of eyes, watching every move you make. There's also the possibility that someone may not like your speech. They're easy to spot. Either they're snoring, fidgeting, looking down on the floor or staring at you with vacant eyes. They're the ones who sit in stony silence while everyone else is laughing and having a good time. It's tempting for an inexperienced speaker to try and win them over. I was thinking about that when the club president gently nudged me.

He leaned over as if to whisper in my ear. This time, I backed away causing his face to crumble into an embarrassed grin. "Oops, I'm sorry, I forgot! I'm going to introduce you now," he said.

After a few introductory remarks myself, I launched into my speech, paraphrasing the following Blue Ribbon story:

WHO I AM MAKES A DIFFERENCE STORY™

By: Helice "Sparky" Bridges

DifferenceMakersInternational.org

Published in *Chicken Soup for the Soul* — Made into a television movie

A teacher in New York decided to honor each of her high school seniors for the difference they made in her life. Then she presented each of them with a Blue Ribbon imprinted with gold letters, which read, "Who I Am Makes A Difference."™

Afterwards the teacher gave each of the students three more ribbons to acknowledge others to see what impact it would have in their community. They were to follow up on the results, see who honored whom and report back to the class the following week.

One of the students honored a junior executive in a nearby company for helping him with his career planning. The student gave him a blue ribbon and put it on his shirt just over his heart. Then the boy gave him two extra ribbons, explained their class project on acknowledgement and enlisted the executive's help.

Later that day the junior executive went to his boss and told him that he deeply admired him for being a creative genius. The junior executive asked him if he would accept the gift of the blue ribbon and would he give him permission to put it on him. His surprised boss said, "Well, sure." After placing the ribbon above his boss' heart, he asked him to support the efforts of the class project and pass on the extra ribbon.

That night the grouchy boss went home to his 14-year-old son and sat him down. He said, "The most incredible thing happened to me today. I was in my office and one of the junior executives came in and told me he admired me and gave me this blue ribbon for being a creative genius. Imagine. He

thinks I'm a creative genius. Then he put this blue ribbon that says 'Who I Am Makes A Difference'™ on my jacket above my heart. Next he gave me an extra ribbon and asked me to find somebody else to honor. As I was driving home tonight, I started thinking about whom I would honor with this ribbon and I thought about you, son. I want to honor you."

"My days are really hectic and when I come home I don't pay a lot of attention to you. Sometimes I scream at you for not getting good enough grades in school or for your bedroom being a mess. But somehow tonight, I just wanted to sit here and, well, just let you know that you do make a difference to me. Besides your mother, you are the most important person in my life. You're a great kid and I love you!"

The startled boy started to sob and sob, and he couldn't stop crying. His whole body shook. He walked over to a drawer, pulled out a gun, stared at his father and, through his tears said, "I was planning on committing suicide tomorrow, Dad, because I didn't think you loved me. Now I don't need to."

Copyright © Helice Bridges

Be a steward of the dream…A Blue Ribbon Over the Hearts of 300 Million people by the year 2020
Contact us to make a difference: OFFICE: 760-753-0963
www.DifferenceMakersInternational.org, EMAIL: info@blueribbons.org

The story impacted almost everyone in the restaurant that night, especially the club president. There was not one dry eye in the room.

I wrapped up by reminding everyone that they could be making a difference in someone else's life without even knowing it. Then I sat down, fully satisfied with my speech. The club president picked up the wooden hammer and banged against the gong, drawing the meeting to a close.

Looking out the window, I saw to my dismay that it was pouring. Heavy rain was cascading down the windows. The raindrops were illuminated by the street lights outside. Mumbling under my breath, I said, "Darn, I'm going to get drenched!"

Someone tugged at my sleeve. I turned around to find the club president hovering over me. He asked if I wanted a ride to the subway station, which I gratefully accepted.

Fortunately his umbrella was large enough to cover us both on the way to his car. As we pulled away, he drove slowly, as if he didn't want to drop me off so soon. Something was on his mind. He appeared to be deep in thought, as if he were trying to figure out what to say.

Finally, he switched on the night light (it was totally dark by that point), and said, "Your speech about making a difference really hit me hard tonight. Thank you for coming out to share that story with us."

He continued, "It made me realize that I've never told my sons how much I love them. Because of you, I'm going to sit them down tonight and tell them exactly that. Thank you!"

It was a stunning statement. There I was, a fledgling speaker, already making a difference on a set of boys I would never get to meet.

We arrived at the subway station a few minutes later. Before getting out of the car, I turned to face him.

"Your boys will forever remember what you're about to tell them tonight."

Tears were streaming down his face. I gave him a bear hug, squeezed his hand one final time, and lumbered out of the car.

Standing on the curb, I watched the taillights fade into the night. Once he turned the corner and was out of sight, I realized I was shivering uncontrollably in the pouring rain. I ran for cover underground and caught the subway home.

I never found out what happened after that night. I can only surmise those boys were forever changed.

Food for Thought: Never underestimate the fact that you are making a difference whether or not you're aware of it.

EXERCISE – CHAPTER FIFTEEN

Each of you has a divinely appointed purpose while here on Earth and yours is as unique as a snowflake. Like Mrs. Jordan, the fifth grade teacher who had no earthly idea that she transformed a little boy's life, you've also touched other people's lives without even knowing it. Sometimes we find out later because either the person who was affected told you or someone else made that observation and shared those thoughts with you.

Write down what you did for someone else that turned out to be a big deal for that person. How did it make you feel?

Let's turn this around. Describe something someone did for you that made such a big impact on your life in ways that you never anticipated. What was it that this person did and how did it transform your life? You see? It works both ways!

SIXTEEN
GOODBYE WALL STREET!

One day in 1996, in the middle of a particularly busy trading day, I made arrangements to fly out to Florida for a badly needed winter break. Eager to recharge my batteries and get away from the daily hustle and bustle of Wall Street, I couldn't wait for the cool ocean mist to dampen my hair (I had gobs of it back then) and to feel the hot toasty sand beneath my feet.

The first morning there, I hurriedly ate a low-fat breakfast of yogurt, banana and coffee, then headed straight for the beach. I took with me my usual beach paraphernalia, including a bottle of tanning lotion, an extra large beach towel and a good spiritual book. After finding myself a lounge chair, I plopped down for a full day of relaxation.

The combination of an engrossing book and the tantalizing feel of the hot sun against my pale winter skin made me comfortably drowsy. Everything in my body let go and melted into nothingness. Thoughts of the stock market quickly faded, and I soon lost all track of time.

Drifting further away from reality, my eyes grew heavier with each passing minute. No longer did I feel the weight of the book sitting on top of my chest, which rose and fell with every breath

I took. A gentle breeze picked up now and then to brush against my moist forehead, giving me a cool sensation. Images began to form and solidify. Characters swam into focus. They were all talking to each other and to me. My mouth opened and closed as if on autopilot, while bits of saliva involuntarily slid down my chin.

Then it happened.

A thought suddenly thundered in my head, shoving aside those dream characters like a tidal wave, stunning me with its forceful impact. Jolted out of my stupor, my eyes flew open. Bolting upright, I unconsciously wiped my mouth with the back of my hand and blinked against the harsh sun. I looked around to see if I was imagining things.

Rubbing my eyes vigorously, it took a full moment to realize that I had just heard a voice in my head—from God. It was crystal clear, even though it made no sense at the time. I again looked around to see if anyone was near me who was perhaps trying to speak into a deaf man's ear, but I was virtually alone on the beach that morning.

What I heard was that I was to become a transformational speaker and author whose mission was to touch countless people's lives and help them make the shift to achieving their own dreams. My newfound mission, according to this voice, was to help people integrate their lives with the divine, the infinite creative organizing power of all aspects of creation, which exists in the entire universe, from the microscopic to the macroscopic.

What was so strange about this experience is that, although I had not spoken to a live audience in a long while or published anything under my name, I just *knew that I was supposed to move in that direction.* I seemed to have an inner knowingness that, despite my stupendous success on Wall Street, buying and selling stocks was not really my divine purpose—more like a pit stop on the way to my destiny.

Now, every single cell in my body was vibrating. Never before had I felt so totally alive—I absolutely could not wait to go back to New York City and begin laying the groundwork for this transition to happen! It had to be the voice of God.

Despite the rousing excitement, I had plenty of doubts along the way. My ego began bombarding me with thoughts that I was crazy for giving up such a lucrative career. It did not like the idea of possibly going back to peanut butter and jelly sandwiches for dinner.

But eight months later, I cleaned out my office and bid farewell to everyone. Walking across the marble lobby of the Merrill Lynch building on Fifth Avenue for the last time on December 23, 1996, I remember thinking I had no idea what would become of my future. But I walked out with my back straight and head up high, determined to trust the unknown.

Food for Thought: Trust that bigger things are in store for you if you listen to your intuition, take action and believe that things will work out despite lack of clear supporting evidence.

EXERCISE – CHAPTER SIXTEEN

This chapter was about remaining open to intuitive urgings. You've had more than one occasion where your higher self was telling you to follow a certain path or you somehow knew the answer to something without knowing why. The phone was ringing and you instantly knew who it was or you entered in some kind of contest and something told you that you'd win first place. That happened to me when I was competing in a Toastmasters Humorous Speech contest several years ago. The moment they began announcing first, second and third place winners, I instantly knew I had won first place and I did!

Listening to your intuition is the greatest gift you can give yourself. It's the same thing as opening a communication channel with your higher self. Inside you there's a huge reservoir of creative intelligence that has the answer to everything you've ever wanted to know. The problem in today's world is that many of us tend to get caught up with the fast pace of life and we forget to stop and reconnect.

I'd like to invite you to go for a walk in the woods or in the park if you live in a metropolitan city. While on your walk, ponder those times when you listened to your intuition and were glad you did. Write down a few of those instances and then think about those times when you knew you should have paid attention to your gut feelings but went and did the opposite thing. What happened as a result?

PART IV

LEARNING TO TRUST

SEVENTEEN
THE $9.99 SOUP

Taking a leap of faith and leaving my rewarding job on Wall Street led me to one of the hardest times of my life. My finances quickly hit a low point, as I plowed through most of my savings to pay down some debt and other obligations. Interestingly though, it also turned out to be one of the best times of my life, because I discovered that it didn't take very much for me to survive.

One day on a hot and muggy Saturday in New York City, I went to a seminar for the local chapter of the National Speakers Association, of which I was a member. A guest speaker from out of town had been invited to speak at the seminar, which was scheduled to go from nine to five.

At noon, we were given an hour lunch break. Not wanting to walk through horribly muggy conditions, I decided to stay inside the hotel and have lunch at the air-conditioned restaurant on the first floor.

Not surprisingly, almost everything on the menu was priced at $18.99 or higher. The problem was I only had $10 on me—my last $10.

I struggled with the decision: To eat or not to eat? But ravenously hungry, I knew I had to eat. I also had tremendous faith; I had always experienced that I never had to worry about having my basic needs met, even when I didn't know where my next paycheck would be coming from. The universe had always provided for me.

I ordered the cheapest item on the menu: a cream of broccoli soup for only $9.99. While it temporarily wiped away hunger pangs, I jammed my pockets with free crackers in case I got hungry later. When one of my colleagues asked why I was only having a bowl of soup for lunch, I simply told him I wasn't very hungry, too embarrassed to say that I didn't have enough money for more.

When the seminar was finally over, I went home and headed straight to the mailbox to find a hefty stack of mail waiting for me. Wedged among the letters and ads was a flaming red envelope that immediately grabbed my attention. Pulling it out from the middle of the stack, I examined it with curiosity. There was no return address on it. Intrigued, I ripped it open and something fell out. It floated down to the floor like a butterfly in slow motion. Mesmerized, I stared at it.

Was this a dream? Was this really happening?

As soon as I came to my senses, I quickly scooped it up. It was a crisp $10 bill.

Surprised to get cash in the mail like that, I reached back inside the red envelope and pulled out a form letter. It was from a company bribing me to fill out a survey.

Hey, you just paid for my lunch today; sure no problem! I thought.

Then it hit me: Who says the universe can't handle small details?

Food for Thought: It's the universe's job to take care of you— if you let it.

EXERCISE – CHAPTER SEVENTEEN

When was the last time when things mysteriously fell into place without so much effort on your part? It has happened more than you realize. When you are in sync with life, enormous possibilities emerge for you.

Can you think of a time in your life when you had absolutely no idea how you were going to come up with the money to pay for something and then the money mysteriously showed up? Maybe you received an unexpected inheritance from a long lost relative or the bank made an error on your account and gave you a credit adjustment.

Sometimes it's not money you think you're lacking. Let's say you wanted to accomplish a certain task but you had no idea how you'd do it yet someone showed up at the right time to guide you. Perhaps you overheard snippets of a conversation in a busy coffee shop, read a newspaper article or heard something on the radio that gave you the answer you were looking for. Too often people chalk this up to "coincidence" when in fact they're not.

Pinpoint one or two situations in your life where something like the above happened to you. What were your thoughts or feelings at the time? Did you take inspired action to fulfill the task?

EIGHTEEN
TALE OF THE LOST DRIVER'S LICENSE

Getting around New York City was really easy. Back in those days (1982-1998), I had a choice between walking, taking the subway, hailing a cab or riding my bike. There was no need for a car.

So when I somehow lost my driver's license during the early eighties, I wasn't concerned. I assumed that when the expiration date drew near, the Department of Motor Vehicles would automatically send me a renewal form. Had I bothered to check, I would have known that this was my responsibility, not theirs.

My thinking at the time was: "Who needs a car in Manhattan when it's virtually impossible to find yourself a place to park, and when you're lucky enough to find one, you ran the risk of being ticketed for some ridiculous parking violation that no one knew about?"

What I didn't know was that if your license was not renewed within a certain time frame, New York State law required that you go through the entire process of applying for a new one all over again. That meant getting your eyes checked, attending several weeks of drivers education class, taking a written multiple choice test and then going through a road examination. All of that could take weeks, if not months! I felt defeated before I even started.

But one day, I felt a strong impulse (intuition) to get my affairs in order, and that included getting a new driver's license. On the face of it, there was no obvious reason to do it because I wasn't planning on moving out of the city anytime soon. So I ignored the invisible nudge and let several more weeks pass without taking action. But the longer I ignored that feeling, the stronger it got, to the point where it literally became a waking obsession.

With great reluctance, I finally signed up for drivers education during the winter of 1996-1997. After completing all of the required classes and acing the written exam, a road test was scheduled for January 1997.

On the assigned day, I arrived at the designated testing location somewhere in Brooklyn to find a small cluster of people, mostly high school boys and girls, impatiently withstanding sub-zero temperatures. In my thirties at the time, I easily was the oldest applicant on hand.

After waiting for what seemed like hours, I was relieved when a small black four-door Nissan with "Department of Motor Vehicles" emblazoned on the side made its way over to us.

"Oh my God, I hope I go first, I'm freezing to death," I mumbled to no one in particular.

Unfortunately, the examiner seemed in no hurry to gather her paperwork, made what was probably an unnecessary cell phone call, and slowly sloshed her way through the wet snow to where all of us were standing on the sidewalk. She took a roll call, mumbling off a litany of names. Furrowing my eyebrows and zeroing in on her lips, I inched a little closer and waited for my name to be called.

Finally, she blurted out something that vaguely looked familiar.

"Hopson, where is Mr. Hopson?"

My hand shot up. "Here!"

As soon as the last name on the list rolled off her tongue, I approached the examiner to make her aware of my deafness situation. Memories of the "James Bond Lady" fiasco were still fresh in my mind.

"Um, I just want to make you aware that I'm hearing impaired and read lips. Okay?"

She replied, "Well, Mr. Hopson, it just so happens that you are the first on my list for today's road test. Shall we?" For some reason, she eyed me suspiciously and pointed to the government-issued car with a smirk on her face.

The first thing she said to me once we were inside the car was "Mr. Hopson, the first thing you're going to do is parallel paahhk. Only three reverses are allowed."

Pointing up ahead, she continued, "Please drive up the road here and paahhk right between those two cars."

I felt as if I were sixteen all over again.

Somehow I managed to squeeze between two abandoned cars, and then we were off, making left and right turns and stops along the way or whatever she directed me to do. At one point, we drove through what looked like a drug-infested neighborhood. I found myself briefly wondering what I'd do if we were suddenly caught in a hail of gunfire between rival neighborhood gangs. Dancing in my head were fantasies of suddenly becoming a hero for bravely driving through a fierce gang gunfight: *Man Taking Road Exam Saves D.O.T. Examiner's Life.*

Snapping back to reality, I noticed she was impatiently ordering me to get on the highway for some real-world cruising.

We were back in less than an hour. Shutting down the engine,

I turned sideways and was surprised to find her lips peeled back, revealing pearly white teeth. The change of demeanor was a welcome sight.

Handing me a slip of paper, she exclaimed, "Congratulations, Mr. Hopson you'll be receiving your driver's license in a couple of weeks!" I was giddy with delight.

Six months later, a new opportunity came my way to work on a book project in another state almost a thousand miles away. What do you need in order to move out of the city into the suburbs?

Exactly.

Food for Thought: God has a plan for everyone. Trust that He knows what you need to do next. It's up to you to heed inner impulses and take spontaneous right action. The rest will fall into place effortlessly.

OBSTACLE ILLUSIONS

EXERCISE – CHAPTER EIGHTEEN

One of my favorite jokes goes something like this: "How do you get God to laugh?" The answer: "Tell Him your plans." Pretty funny huh?

Even the best-laid plans go awry. Unfortunately we live in a culture that teaches us to be in control of every aspect of our lives.

When we are willing to listen and surrender, nature will guide you to take spontaneous right action that will be the perfect solution for you.

If I hadn't listened to my higher self in this story, I'm sure I would have eventually gotten the license renewed but the universe wanted me to be ready for when the opportunity came to move to another state. Imagine the delay that would have happened had I not renewed the license at that time – I would have had to put off the opportunity that came to me, perhaps closing that window.

Was there a time when you felt compelled to take a certain course of action but you didn't know why only to find out later the reason(s)?

NINETEEN
THE GROCERY BILL

As I noted earlier, the decision to leave Wall Street and begin a new career led me to one of the most challenging times of my life. Indeed, this life-altering change caused me to pay a heavy price.

One morning, the empty refrigerator and cupboards told me it was time to go shopping again. After making an ATM cash withdrawal of $40, I headed to the nearest supermarket, eight long city blocks away.

Arriving at the store twenty minutes later, I grabbed a cart and went food shopping. I spent over an hour mentally calculating how much the contents of my grocery cart would add up to. After walking up and down the aisles and carefully selecting my food for the week, I was finally done. I approached the first available checkout lane.

The teenaged gum-popping cash register boy with curly brown hair greeted me with a bored expression, "How ya doing?" He was totally oblivious to me. Ringing up item after item was just a clock-punching job to him. My eyes, on the other hand, were anxiously riveted on the cash register, hoping $40 would be enough.

The total came to exactly $39.99.

While drowning in excitement over the fact that I had just enough money for groceries, I had completely forgotten that the penny I got back was in no way going to cover the cost of a cab ride back to my apartment. But as soon as I stepped into the sweltering heat outside, my hand automatically shot up to flag down a cab. That's when I remembered.

"Sorry, I changed my mind" I said with an embarrassed grin to a cab driver who had just pulled up alongside me.

Eight long blocks.

Gritting my teeth, I grabbed five heavy bags in each hand and started the long trek back home. Between the intense heat and the frustration of not having enough money for a cab, I began muttering a litany of expletives. By the time I arrived at the curb to begin the walk uptown, sweat was cascading down my face.

Angrily setting the bags down and furiously rubbing my reddened hands, I took a swig of cold bottled water, thinking how many more blocks were left.

Suddenly, my mind began to swirl with images of starving children I had recently seen, completely throwing me for a loop. I couldn't shake one particular image of a heart-breaking scene of a starving child collapsed on the ground, struggling to get to a food center during a famine in Africa. In the background, a vulture sat, watching the emaciated child who was surrounded by thousands of black flies. The ghastly scene instantly changed my attitude.

Flooded with renewed gratitude, I looked up at the sky, said a silent prayer and made the rest of the way home without further incident.

Food for Thought: An attitude of gratitude will get you through virtually anything.

EXERCISE – CHAPTER NINETEEN

One of the greatest secrets of life is having an attitude of gratitude. Years ago when I was doing some serious introspection work, I was introduced to this wonderful concept by a best-selling author named Sarah Ban Breathnach who created a lovely gratitude journal for her readers to write five things to be grateful for everyday. This deceptively simple yet powerful technique has helped millions of people shift their focus from a life of insufficiency to one of sufficiency. They're able to focus on what they have, not what they don't have.

The more you put your attention on something, the more it expands, whether it's good or bad. That's natural law. If you're constantly dwelling on how you don't have enough money in the bank or how you're always suffering from one ailment or another, then that's what the universe will keep bringing you until you decide to change your focus.

I invite you to buy yourself a nice journal and get into the habit of writing at least 3 to 5 things you're grateful for the next 30 days and watch what happens. Use the space below to get started.

TWENTY
FIRST CAR LOAN

Being upfront about something in order to get what we want can take tremendous courage. Sometimes it requires that we divulge information we'd prefer to keep private because we think it might put us in a vulnerable position.

This happened to me when I applied for my very first car loan in 1998, after moving 1,000 miles away from New York City to work on the book project I mentioned at the end of Chapter 18 that I was invited to take part in.

After a few car dealerships turned me down for a loan, I was at my wit's end. I knew what the problem was: during the early eighties I had been careless with credit cards and ended up tarnishing my credit history. By the time I went looking for my first car, I was still in the process of cleaning up the mess I had made.

When I confided in a colleague about my situation, he gave me the name of a large Dodge dealership from where he had previously purchased a Jeep. I was on my way in a flash, hoping for the best.

Upon setting foot inside the showroom, I was met by a young, enthusiastic salesman named Jeff. He appeared fresh out of college, eager to make a sale. What he didn't know was that moments before arriving at the dealership, I had had an overwhelming urge to be upfront about my bad credit situation.

As soon as we sat down, I immediately launched into the "bad debt story." Watching his smile disappear and shoulders slump almost made me regret what I was doing. But it was too late—I pressed on and left nothing out.

I'm sure the young salesman thought I was a lost cause, but to his credit, he said he would do what he could and politely asked me to fill out the necessary paperwork. He took my application and disappeared into the back offices, probably to tell the sales manager what a sorry case I was. He said he'd be back in a jiffy.

While waiting for him to return, I looked around the showroom and spotted a distinguished-looking salesman at his desk. There was something magical about his appearance and his mannerisms. For some inexplicable reason, I felt compelled to speak with him.

Glancing in the direction where Jeff had previously made his exit and not seeing him anywhere, I decided to walk over and introduce myself to him. Stopping a few feet away from his desk, my eyes were drawn to his nameplate.

Mr. Shoebottom.

What a strange name, I thought. *His name sounds like something right out of a storybook.*

Mr. Shoebottom was on the phone. Seeing that I was waiting for him to finish, he covered the mouthpiece and whispered, "I'll be right with you."

Not wanting to distract him, I went for a little walk around the showroom, all the while keeping an eye on him. As soon as he hung up, I intended to dash back over before his phone had a chance to ring again.

Finally, he stood up and waved to me. Glancing in the direction where the young salesman had been and seeing that he still hadn't returned, I quickly darted over to Mr. Shoebottom's desk.

The friendly salesman reached out and firmly shook my hand, asking, "Sir, how may I help you?"

Peeking down at his nameplate to make sure I wasn't imagining things, I said, "Mr. Shoebottom, my name is Stephen Hopson, and I'm here to buy a car for the first time in my life. A friend of mine recommended your dealership, which is why I'm here. I filled out some paperwork and gave it to Jeff over there for processing. But, there's one problem."

"And what might that be?" he said with a slight air of detachment, as if he heard this all the time.

I pushed on, "Sir, I messed up my credit during the early eighties, and although I've been cleaning it up the last few years, you guys might find my credit check to be unfavorable. To be honest with you, I'm a little worried about it."

His face immediately changed from the detached, businesslike expression to one of genuine understanding. The sudden transformation took me aback. I remember thinking I must have triggered something inside him. What it was, I didn't know, but I would find out a few days later.

"Please have a seat. I'll go see how Jeff is doing with your paperwork. I'll be right back."

It wasn't long before Mr. Shoebottom returned with the young salesman in tow. He was beaming, as if he'd just made the biggest sale of the month.

"Mr. Hopson, your car loan was approved. Congratulations!"

It took me a second to gather my wits.

Not believing my eyes (remember, I lip-read) I said,

"WHAT!?!? I don't need a cosigner or anything?"

"Your report did not have any history of bad credit," said Mr. Shoebottom. He was beaming like a proud father.

A million thoughts ran through my head. If my credit was so good, then how come the previous three dealerships had turned me down for a loan earlier that week?

It didn't make any sense.

I was reminded of a quote from Joel Osteen's best-selling book, *Your Best Life Now*:

"God's favor is opening doors of opportunity. His favor is bringing success in your life. His favor is causing people to make exceptions for you."

When I went back to pick up my shiny new purple Dodge Neon a couple of days later, I was dying to ask the man with the storybook name what had really happened.

With a warm, knowing smile, he said, "Several years ago, I experienced a very bad bankruptcy and know first-hand what it is like to be denied a loan because of bad credit. I did not want that to happen to you."

Food for Thought: If you take a big risk and be upfront about your personal situation, the universe may reward you in surprising ways!

EXERCISE – CHAPTER TWENTY

I've learned that being transparent pays off huge dividends whether you're applying for a loan or conducting business.

As a transformational speaker, my audiences expect no less from me. When I'm up there on the platform, I have a huge responsibility to bring forth ideas and concepts that have the potential to truly transform lives but if I try to be someone else then the message gets lost. The audience subconsciously turns a deaf ear.

One time I was giving a speech to a packed room of business executives when in the middle of my talk my mind suddenly went blank. I had walked away from the podium where my notes were. At first I grew nervous at the prospect of acting like nothing happened but then just as quickly I smiled and admitted that I had forgotten what I wanted to say and walked back to the podium to check my notes. They all laughed appreciatively and I gained a few new fans that night.

Let me ask you this – who would you be more inspired by – someone who appears to be super polished or one who acts from a place of integrity? Write about those times when you were acting from both places and how it affected you and others around you.

TWENTY ONE
BLIZZARD HOUSECLEANING

A friend and I had driven two hundred miles without incident while traveling from upstate New York to Michigan after the Christmas holidays sometime during the late 1990s. At one point, we decided to stop at a gas station in a tiny rural town in Canada. It was time for coffee and a quick rest stop.

Climbing out of the car, I looked up at the sky and saw that it was dark, ominous, almost foreboding. The air was uncomfortably damp, and it was drizzling lightly. I felt chilled to the bones.

I quickly went inside to use the restroom and scurried back to the warm car. Even though the gas tank was only half-empty, I felt a strong urge to refill it. Normally, I would have waited until the empty fuel gauge flashed me a warning sign. But, I filled it up, paid for it with a credit card, and sped back to the freeway.

Within minutes, it began to snow. It had been a long time since snow had fallen, so I was delighted. At first it came down lightly, but before I realized what was happening, the snow began to swirl down harder and harder, quickly cutting visibility. I was forced to slow the car to a crawl. My stomach tightened for the first time that night.

Roads were fast turning to ice, and the wind blew harder with each passing minute. The wind was so strong that I felt as if I were piloting a small aircraft through severe turbulence. We had to find a hotel—fast.

Eventually my friend and I saw what we both thought was a sign for hotel accommodations right before an exit. The whiteout conditions made it exceedingly difficult for us to see the sign clearly, but we decided to take a chance and got off the freeway.

The ramp led us to a T intersection with a yellow blinking traffic light swinging wildly in the wind. It was either right or left. Straight ahead was nothing but acres of wilderness. While contemplating the next course of action, I felt a light tap on my shoulder. My friend was pointing to the left. There was a lone car a few miles down the road.

Hoping they were from the area, we decided to follow them. But in less than three minutes we realized they were just as lost as we were! We had no choice but to head back the way we came, desperately hoping we would find a hotel.

Turning the car around on the treacherously narrow two-lane road proved to be tricky. The wind was howling menacingly all around us. The possibility of being windswept into the ditches was real—*very* real. With the greatest concentration I could muster, I took a deep breath and swung the car back and forth, inches at a time, in an attempt to carefully turn the car around without sliding into the ditch.

Suddenly the rear wheels spun like crazy, sinking the car deeper into the snow.

I felt a sense of panic rising up from within. It was a sickening feeling. Scared out of my wits, I nervously continued to rock the tiny car in a rhythmic fashion until the wheels finally caught and miraculously lurched us forward with a jolt.

Thank God.

As we headed in the opposite direction, my heart pounded wildly. Hunched over the steering wheel and squinting my eyes even harder, I tried to see through the howling blizzard to find the ramp, but it was virtually impossible to see where I was going.

There was no sign of life anywhere. We were alone on this road—the taillights of the other car had long disappeared into the blackness in the opposite direction. We decided to try to find the freeway again, where we'd search for an overpass for temporary shelter, at least until the storm blew over.

Suddenly realizing that we might be low on gas, I looked at the gas gauge, hoping against hope that we had a decent amount of gas left.

Incredibly, it was still full! Thank God I had followed my hunch to get gas earlier.

In the midst of all this, I remembered I was carrying in my right pocket a small, smooth stone with FAITH inscribed across the surface. My right hand shook as I reached down to touch it. Wrapping my hand around it, I briefly stopped the car, closed my eyes and fervently prayed, *"Dear God, please get us back on the freeway. Please guide us home now."*

When I opened my eyes, I let out a gasp. Somehow we had made it to the freeway entrance! We must have been there all along, but perhaps we couldn't see it because it was snowing so hard? I'm not really sure what happened, but there we were, right where we wanted to be!

Clutching the steering wheel, I slowly drove up the icy ramp, completely relying on the small yellow reflectors along the edge of the roadside that shimmered in the glare of the car's headlights. They shone like beacons, steadily guiding me to freedom, and it wasn't long before we were finally back on the freeway, driving at a snail's pace for the longest time.

A few hours later we saw several powerful beams of light illuminating the night sky about eight miles away. It resembled a small, bustling city. My friend and I looked at each other, relieved.

"We'll pull off up there and find a hotel for the night," I said happily.

But as we got closer, we saw it wasn't a city after all—it was a bunch of cars and trucks stuck in the ditches on both sides of the road, with their headlights crisscrossing the snowy night sky!

At that moment, I realized just how close we had come to the same perilous situation. As we continued down the highway, past and current problems totally vanished from my mind. I found myself mentally forgiving everyone who had "wronged" me in the past, clearing out the tangle of past memories that no longer served me.

Never before had I done so much mental housecleaning! All I could think about was how I wanted to live from now on. It helped me to stay focused on our survival and getting home alive.

Nine excruciating hours later, we saw the most beautiful sign we had ever seen: *BRIDGE TO USA, 27 MILES.*

Food for Thought: Who says the universe doesn't know how to give you good cause for mental housecleaning? It even paid for the gas. The charge never showed up on my credit card!

EXERCISE – CHAPTER TWENTY ONE

Like what happened with the bully on the school playground so many years ago and then the terrifying drive through the blizzard, we are given opportunities to test our inner strength at seemingly inopportune times.

Can you recall one or two events where you got so scared but you somehow ended up not only getting through the ordeal in one piece but also became stronger because of it? Use this space to write a short summary of that and then share something you hadn't known about yourself. Did it surprise you that you "had it in you all along"?

PART V

THE SKY'S THE LIMIT!

TWENTY TWO
THE JOVIAL FLIGHT INSTRUCTOR

While putting final touches to this book, I learned that a man who had played an integral role in helping me make my flying dreams come true had passed away of a brain aneurysm. The news greatly saddened me, but I knew he would not have wanted any of us to mourn his death, but rather celebrate his life.

Other than my fifth-grade teacher and my parents, this man touched me in ways very few people have. Like Mrs. Jordan, he believed in my dreams. He believed that he could teach me, a deaf man, how to fly. This is the story of how he gave me the key to unlocking my aviation dreams.

Around 1999, I was still in the process of building my inspirational speaking and writing career, which meant I had to find myself a part-time job to pay the bills in between engagements.

At that point, I was already two months into private pilot flight training at Macomb New Haven flight school in Michigan. When the instructor had to close down his one-man operation to take a flying job in Colorado, I was forced to find a new instructor elsewhere. It was not easy to try and convince ignorant flight instructors that deaf pilots can fly and have, in fact, been flying since the 1940s.

But I would not be deterred.

Let's rewind to my childhood for a moment, and to Chapter Four, where I first mentioned my childhood dream of flying one day. When I was four years old, I remember often looking up at the sky and wanting to "fly with the big boys." My parents, not knowing any better, often admonished me to be realistic: "Stephen, be realistic! You're deaf. Deaf people can't fly airplanes! Now stop this nonsense right now!"

Despite their admonitions, I begged my mother to take me to the airport so that I could experience the excitement I always felt around planes. I finally wore her down to the point where she agreed to take me to Albany County Airport once a week, usually on the weekends. It was one of my most treasured childhood activities—we'd watch planes take off and land for hours. I couldn't get enough of it.

The moment she'd pull up to the fence that surrounded the perimeter of the airport, I'd be out of the car in a flash and wrap my tiny hands around the wires of the fence, peering through whatever hole gave me the best view of the airport. Then I'd wait with delicious anticipation.

As soon as I saw a plane heading for the takeoff runway, I would run back to the hood of my mother's car, carefully lay my head down and wait for what I always knew was coming. It never failed. The plane would roar down the runway and lift majestically into the air, causing the tiny car to vibrate like a washing machine. It made my day!

I don't recall how long we kept up this weekly ritual, but shortly after I first got my driver's license, I took my dream of flying even further. Whenever the mood struck, I'd go for a long drive in the country and, after making sure there was no other traffic around, swing over to the middle of the highway and pretend I was taking off and landing, all the while watching the broken white lines disappear beneath me. I'd be pushing all sorts of imaginary buttons on the dashboard and act as if I were talking on the radio to air traffic controllers. It was a blast!

One day this exercise felt so real that I had to pull off to the side to cry tears of joy. Despite evidence to the contrary, somehow I knew right then and there that one day I would be a pilot, regardless of what my parents or other people thought.

Now back to the future. After 15 years of working on Wall Street and relocating halfway across the country, I found myself sitting in front of my computer one Saturday morning, surfing the Internet, when I suddenly came upon a website that I never knew existed.

It was created by and for deaf pilots!

Stunned, I literally froze in place, staring at the website's home page, not believing what I was seeing. My childhood dreams, long forgotten, came roaring back with a vengeance. When I returned to the present, I knew it was time for me to take the next step: find a flight instructor.

That's how I found Jason, my first flight instructor, who operated the one-man flight school at Macomb-New Haven, a small airport a short distance from my home. Although he thought people with a hearing impairment were not allowed to fly, once I provided ample evidence to the contrary, he decided to give me a chance and take me on as a new student pilot. Unfortunately, our student-teacher relationship was short-lived because of that flying job I mentioned earlier.

While looking for a new flight instructor, it occurred to me that I probably should get a part-time job at whatever airport I ended up going to complete my flight training. Why not? It made sense.

After visiting a handful of airports throughout the area and learning that nothing was available, I ventured a little further out and found Oakland/Troy airport. It was nestled in a fast growing metropolitan area (Troy, Michigan), with several strip malls, modern apartments, a giant Wal-Mart superstore, and an assortment of office and industrial buildings. The only area with wide-open space nearby was a small golf course just to the west of the airport. The runway was long enough to accommodate small jets, but the amount of daily traffic did not justify the expense of building an air traffic control tower.

Perfect.

Now all I needed was to find myself a job and a new flight instructor at this place.

Pulling into the newly repaved parking lot, I noticed a small circular white terminal building up ahead.

That must be where the personnel department is, I thought.

My curiosity led me inside the round building, where I was surprised to see only a handful of people milling around inside the sun-drenched terminal. Some were reading the morning newspaper, while others were helping themselves to a cup of coffee. A large jovial-looking man who looked like he might have been a quarterback at one time was pouring himself a hot cup of coffee. His cheeks were rosy and his demeanor happy-go-lucky.

Seeing a new face, he promptly set down his coffee mug and came barreling toward me with an outstretched hand, startling me. After regaining my composure, I made the mistake of accepting his bone-crushing handshake, causing me to wince. Trying to hide my pained expression, I introduced myself and told him I was looking for the personnel department.

"And I'm Don Solms," he boomed. He was still pumping my now lifeless hand.

Finally releasing his death grip, he said, "Oh, so you want a job here?" His face brightened considerably.

"Yeah, do you know if they have any openings?" I was trying to massage my sore hand, opening and closing it repeatedly.

"I think they might be looking for someone. HEY, let me take you over to the other building and introduce you to Susan. She's the personnel director around here. COME ON!" He was like the overly enthusiastic kid trying to befriend a newcomer on the playground.

Just before I went inside her office, Don shoved his business card inside my shirt pocket and said cheerfully, "Good luck. Shoot me an email later. You'll have to come over to my hangar where I keep my plane. Okay?"

Keeping both hands within the safe confines of my pockets, I gratefully replied, "Thanks, Mr. Solms."

Susan then called Carl and Jason into the office, the two young men in charge of running the flight services department. I would later learn that Jason hadn't wanted to hire me; he felt that a deaf person had no business being at an airport (he would later change his mind). But Carl and Susan disagreed—and they had seniority. A few days later, I got the job!

I was now responsible for fueling and towing airplanes, satisfying customer requests and eventually training new line service personnel. It marked the beginning of an incredible four years at that airport.

One breezy and sunny day, Don was doing some paperwork at his hangar, where he kept his prized Skylane (type of Cessna airplane). The hangar door was up, allowing cool air to swirl around inside. It was an open invitation to anyone who happened to come by.

Small airports were like that. Those who owned their own planes and hangars often liked to socialize with other pilots as well as airport personnel. They'd leave their hangar doors wide open, welcoming anyone who wanted to stop in for a friendly chat.

As I made my way back to the terminal after fueling a customer's plane a few hangars away from his, Don waved me in and offered me a cold soda. Not one to resist a thirst quencher, I went inside the hangar and found myself a comfortable chair.

About ten minutes into the conversation, the subject of my flying dreams surfaced. I shared with him how, while trying to earn money, I was in the process of finding myself a new instructor to pick up where I had left off. Before he could respond, the vibrating pager attached to my hip momentarily distracted me with a new text message. It was from the front desk with another fuel order, which meant I had to get going.

"Don, I've gotta go—they're telling me to fuel another plane. We can pick up where we left off later. See ya!"

I was on my way back to the fuel truck when Don startled me by slamming his hand on my right shoulder. As I spun around, my mind flashed back to the day we had met at the terminal. This jovial man had a way of startling people when they least expected it!

Grabbing my arm, he gave it a powerful squeeze. His eyes were sparkling like diamonds. I was in no way prepared for what he was about to say next.

"I would be honored to be your flight instructor, and I won't charge you a dime. All you'd be responsible for is the cost of renting an airplane."

I stood there with my mouth agape, not knowing quite what to say. But one thing I knew for sure was that an angel was present.

Absentmindedly rubbing my arms to stem the tide of goose

bumps, all I could think of saying was, "Wow, really? Oh my God, thanks!"

By this point, my pager was vibrating repeatedly because Patty, the efficient receptionist, was desperately trying to get my attention. I felt pulled in two directions: I wanted to stay and truly enjoy the moment, but at the same time, I felt pressured to get going.

I was about to get in the truck when his face turned serious for a moment and he said, "When are you free for your first lesson?"

The impact of that question caused me to miss the steps of the driver's side, and I almost fell. Grabbing the door handle, I steadied myself and replied, "Well, um, how about tomorrow?" I was certainly not expecting this to happen so quickly!

His eyes shifted upwards as if he had to think for second.

"Okay, we'll start tomorrow!" came the thunderous reply. This was followed by a wink as if he were saying, *This is our secret.*

He was true to his word.

Months of flight training with Don proved to be quite an adventure. He was best known as a jokester, even in the cockpit. So there we were in the small airplane: me, a student pilot, with a 250-pound flight instructor on my right who poked me in the ribs every time he made a joke. I wouldn't have minded if he did that once in a while, but the problem was he thought *everything he said was funny!*

Aside from his dry sense humor, he was one of the most patient flight instructors I would ever have. Every time we got ready for a lesson, he'd explain in the classroom what we were going to do, and then we'd go up and fly. As far as the actual flying was concerned, he never pulled any punches with me. There were no surprises up his sleeves, except for the emergency procedure training we would do later.

If he wanted to explain something to me, he'd tap my arm, and all I had to do was turn quickly to read his lips. But if what he needed to say required more than a few words, he'd take control of the airplane while I focused 100 percent on what he was saying. Then he'd hand over control of the airplane to me. It was that simple.

Don was one of those rare instructors who did not give a hoot about building flight time in hopes of getting an airline job. He was in it for the long haul, which meant I wouldn't have to deal with chronic flight instructor turnover, common throughout the flight training industry.

In fact, it wasn't until after 50 years of instructing that he was forced to hang up his wings in 2006 because of a serious medical problem. That was a sad day for everyone at the airport. No one wanted to see this jovial flight instructor give up his love of flying. It was too painful for them (and me) to watch. He had truly enjoyed the fine art of teaching, and it had showed. He never yelled at his students like some instructors who thought they were drill sergeants in the army. Don treated each student with love and respect. But I'm getting ahead of myself here.

On December 3, 2000 he had a surprise in store for me. We were scheduled to do some practice takeoffs and landings on a calm, sunny day. After doing three of them successfully, he told me to taxi over to the ramp by the white terminal building where we had first met months earlier.

Trying to hide his delight, he said, "Let me see your logbook for a sec." He was grinning like a kid.

Arching my right arm behind the front seats, I snatched the logbook from the bulging black flight bag and tossed it to him, wondering what the jokester was up to this time.

As I watched him flip through the pages of the logbook, it suddenly dawned on me that "today was the day." It was the day every student pilot dreams of. An involuntary shudder raced through my body.

After scribbling his signature in the logbook, he turned and looked at me. His brown eyes were sparkling again. The smile was bigger than ever. Like a child on Christmas morning, Don was positively the giddiest man on the planet at that moment.

"So, Mr. Hopson, *are you ready?*" he boomed happily.

"Yes, Don, get the hell out!" I thundered back, half-joking.

Roaring like a lion, Don heaved his 250-pound football frame out of the airplane, snapped in place the lock of the passenger door and did something that's forever burned in my mind.

He walked around to the front of the airplane and saluted me, like a five-star general sending his young fighter pilots off to war!

I almost burst to tears. No one had ever made such a deeply moving gesture to me. But despite being more than ready to solo that day, I still felt a touch of trepidation and returned the favor with a slightly shaky hand. It was a good thing he was too far away to see that.

After visually checking the sky and making sure no one was coming in for a landing, I swung into position on the runway, took a deep breath and firewalled the throttle. The little plane immediately responded and roared down the runway, literally leaping for joy into the air. I remember thinking, *So this is what everyone meant when they said she'll bounce into the air without your instructor!*

Before long, all the training kicked in, and it was just another exercise around the airport pattern. The only difference was...well, I was *alone*.

After three respectable takeoffs and landings, the venerable flight instructor waved me over and gave me the signal to cut the engine. I was crestfallen. I was having so much fun, I didn't want this to end!

He stood there like a proud papa and, after I shut down the engine, motioned for me to come over to where he was standing. Instead of shaking my hand like I expected, he wrapped his huge arms around me and gave me a bone-crushing hug—but hey, I didn't mind. It was a special moment, that one.

Five months later, exactly one day short of my birthday, he finally authorized me to take a flight test (called "checkride" in aviation terminology) with Mary, a tough but fair-minded FAA examiner based at Pontiac County International airport.

On May 18, 2001, Don and his airplane co-owner Terry accompanied me on a ten-minute flight to Pontiac airport. Besides the fact that I needed Don's help with the radio to get into the tower-controlled airport, they both wanted to be there after the flight test was over.

An hour and a half later, Mary and I landed back at Pontiac. It had been one exhilarating flight test—but I had no clue whether I had passed or not.

As we were taxiing back to the ramp by her office, I was unaware of a radio conversation that was taking place between her and some of my friends back at Oakland/Troy airport. Apparently they had been monitoring the radios, keeping track of my checkride.

When they heard Mary ask the Pontiac tower for permission to land at the airport and taxi back to her office, Jason, the staff member who had thought I didn't have what it took to "make it," put in a radio call to her to ask how my flight test had gone. He was just as anxious, hopeful and excited—if not more than the others—about how I had done!

Later, when we arrived back at Oakland/Troy, he was waiting for me along with the others, beaming. (Ironically, many years later Jason got married and brought into the world a beautiful son who was born with a severe hearing loss. One day he even flew down with his wife to visit me in Ohio, where I had moved, to seek my advice.)

Looking back, I remember Mary turning her head sideways several times while talking on the radio. It never occurred to me that she didn't want me to read her lips, but I later found out that she told them what happened. But I was too busy taxiing the airplane back to her office to really pay much attention anyway.

After the propeller stopped spinning, she opened the door to let cool air inside the cockpit. The moment of truth was coming. I fidgeted nervously, still not knowing whether I had passed or not. Her face gave me no clue.

Pulling out her notes she turned to face me and went over her list, telling me what my strengths and weaknesses were and then suggested ways to improve. She said all of this with a straight face—this lady was all business. I was dying to know if I had passed or failed.

As she neared the end of her list, her face suddenly broke into a sunny smile. "Congratulations, Mr. Hopson, you passed!!"

I wanted to cry, but *not now, not in front of this woman,* I told myself. I fought to hold the tide of emotions that threatened to let loose.

As if on cue, Don and Terry came running out of the building. Apparently they had not heard the radio conversation that had taken place earlier because both of them were gesturing with thumbs up and down motions. Mary reached outside and gave them a solid thumbs up. Don broke into a victory dance while Terry threw both hands in the air.

"It's time for pictures," Terry declared. "You three stand in front of the plane." One of those photos continues to be a treasured piece that I carry with me wherever I go. Every time I look at it, it brings back a flood of pleasant memories.

After we were done, Mary announced to the group, "Let's go inside my office so I can type up Stephen's temporary pilot's license."

Twenty minutes later, the examiner gave me my temporary pilot's license exclaiming, "Once again, congratulations Stephen. You did very well today!"

Standing by the door of her office, Don roared his approval. Terry was giggling.

On our way back out to the airplane, Don turned to me and made a surprise announcement.

"I'll sit in the back. Congratulations Mr. Pilot in Command!"

Once again I fought to stop the tears from flowing. I had a job to do now. Fly them home. It was the most important job I had in the world and one I had dreamt about ever since I was a little boy. I was finally going to be pilot in command, and a couple of people would be relying on my flying skills to get them home safely.

Don believed in me so much that he had told everyone who was willing to listen that I would one day become the first deaf instrument-rated pilot in the world. Six years later, I actually did it, defying every naysayer in the aviation business. Fortunately, Don lived long enough to witness it. He died a year later in 2007 of a brain aneurism.

Thank you, Don, for believing in me.

Food for Thought: Did someone believe in you for something you wanted to achieve? How about turning around and believing in someone else's dreams?

EXERCISE – CHAPTER TWENTY TWO

By now you've probably noticed a powerful theme running throughout this book. There have been more than a few people who appeared on the stage of my life to help me grow.

I know I already asked you to think of those who made a lasting difference in your life but here's another chance to add another person. This time write down the person whose qualities were exactly the opposite of the people you've already written about.

For example, if in the previous exercises you included those whose personalities were positive, think of someone who gave you a hard time, pushed you to the limit or treated you badly all of which resulted in a significant transformation of your life.

TWENTY THREE
THE GREAT ADVENTURE

Deaf pilots have been flying since the late forties. They are not required to use the radio as long as they stay out of controlled airspace. Of the 12,000 airports in America, only 700 have control towers. This leaves us with the option of visiting 11,300 airports throughout America!

When you're out on the road driving, you tend to "see and avoid," right? Pilots operating without the use of a radio, especially deaf pilots, do the exact same thing when taking off, flying enroute and approaching an airport for landing. However, the "see and avoid" concept goes out the window the moment the weather turns sour; only a special group of pilots who have an instrument rating can do this.

These pilots fly their airplanes solely by reference to the instruments to know what the plane is doing, because they have no visual horizon on the outside to guide them. It's like flying through a milk bottle—you're flying blind. Instrument pilots are required to maintain a two-way radio communication under "instrument flying conditions." I actually became the first deaf pilot in the world to obtain that rating, but more on that later.

You may well wonder why anyone would want to spend hours

in a small aircraft, when traveling in a commercial jet would be much faster in most cases. But put yourself in my shoes and imagine you're pilot in command of an aircraft versus a passive passenger on an airline. I can't think of anything that would compare to the thrill of being in charge of a plane hurtling through the sky at 150 miles an hour (or more), flying several thousand feet in the air.

It is definitely not like driving a car, where you navigate via signs posted on the roadside. To aid me with flight navigation, I use an assortment of tools, including an aeronautical chart, a portable GPS unit and other things like a flight plan (a list of alternate airports, various waypoints in the sky, etc.).

While being sole pilot in command of a small plane is beyond thrilling, there are definitely some inconveniences built into it. For instance, you cannot simply pull over if you run out of gas, nor can you respond to Mother Nature (unless you happened to have a special flask aboard for that occasion!).

How does a pilot ensure against running out of fuel? Wind factors, length of flight and fuel burn rates are all taken into consideration when planning a flight prior to departure. Airports along the route are denoted as possible refueling pit stops. Despite the inability to pull over for gas or use the bathroom, hard-core pilots like myself will find every excuse in the book to fly if weather and other factors permit. Trust me, it's a "pilot thing."

Because deaf pilots flying by themselves are unable to use the radio to obtain weather updates, the constantly changing weather provides some challenges for us. We are expected to know where alternate airports are in case we need to make an unscheduled stop due to changing weather conditions. For example, I might be flying along and everything's fine. Visibility is unrestricted, the clouds are high enough and there are no obvious weather problems along the way.

But suddenly I see dark clouds forming on the horizon, something weather forecasters did not expect. What to do? Hearing pilots would call the weather station and obtain an update to determine how to avoid the cloud build-ups. Deaf pilots, on the other hand, have no such luxury. If they feel the quickly changing weather is a threat to their safety, they have no choice but to make an unscheduled landing at one of those alternate airports and wait until the weather clears, while at the same time checking for weather updates via one of the computers at the terminal.

Shortly after receiving my pilot's license in May of 2001, I decided to reward myself by renting a new four-seat airplane and flying myself from Michigan to Kansas City, a 555-mile cross-country trip. The longest flight I had ever done up to that point was my required solo cross-country flight of at least 250 miles, more than halfway through pilot training.

The purpose of this trip was to attend an annual Deaf Pilots' Association fly-in, a small elite group of hearing impaired pilots from around the world. I had never met another deaf pilot, so I was really looking forward to the trip.

Every year this group hosts a week of local sightseeing flights, barbeques and award ceremonies, each of which gives all of us a chance to connect and strengthen our special bond. What made this particular trip even more intriguing was the fact that I would soon be in a room of "flying hands," since many of them communicated through the use of sign language. Imagine—a room full of pilots who sign! Although I didn't become familiar with sign language until I was a sophomore or junior in college, I did become proficient enough to communicate with just about anyone who used it.

On the morning of departure, at exactly 5 a.m., I pulled the plane out of the gigantic hangar, stowed my luggage and got busy. There was a lot to do for the 555-mile cross-country flight. The plane had to be inspected, the fuel tanks topped off and the oil checked. The weather along the route also had to be double-checked (through the use of aviation computers in the weather briefing room). If my flight calculations were correct, it would take me approximately five and a half hours with at least one fuel stop in Illinois.

After the preflight inspection was done, I double-checked the weather one last time and determined the flight was a go. Clear skies with occasional clouds were forecast along the route.

Six hours later, I finally arrived in Kansas, tired but elated. A welcoming committee from the fly-in was on hand to greet me for the first time. It would be the beginning of a long friendship with some of them.

Throughout that week, six or seven of us flew to several towns, including Amelia Earhart's birthplace. We shared the cost of renting the plane, and I enjoyed every minute of our time together, especially the flying part. It helped that we were spared from the thunderstorms Kansas City was known for that summer, making it possible to do almost everything on the schedule. The week flew by all too quickly, and it was soon time to pack up and return home.

The weather forecast for the trip home was to be mostly clear, but I'd also be getting a little extra tailwind, which meant a nice push from Mother Nature. I decided I'd have enough time to extend my fuel stop in Illinois to visit with Clyde, a fellow pilot who lived a stone's throw from the airport.

Clyde and I spent the afternoon catching up and ate a delicious lunch prepared by his wife. Hours later, I glanced at the clock and realized it was getting late. I had to get going because I didn't want to be flying after sunset; I was still a new pilot, and I wasn't comfortable flying alone in the dark. Since it was summer, I had another three hours of daylight left, so I went back to the airport and was soon back in the air, climbing to 7,500 feet and dodging low-level clouds here and there.

For the next two and a half hours, I enjoyed the beautiful summer scenery flowing beneath me. There was no one else up there. Contrary to what many people think, the skies are only potentially crowded when approaching the vicinity of an airport.

According to my GPS, I could see that I was not going to make it to my home airport (Oakland/Troy) before sunset. The sun was fast setting, and I was running out of options. Unless I wanted to continue the flight at night, I had no choice but to land somewhere. Quickly looking through my list of alternate airports, I selected Coldwater Memorial airport, approximately 45 minutes away from my final destination.

Punching the airport's ID into the GPS, I knew I had made a good decision. By the time I got there, the sun would be dipping beneath the horizon. Sure enough, 30 minutes later, I saw the airport's green and white rotating beacon in the distance. Just as I had predicted, the sun was about to slip away.

Circling above the airport to check the position of the orange windsock (to determine wind direction), I made an uneventful landing on the appropriate runway and taxied over to the terminal building, looking for a place to park for the night. My hope had been to sleep on the couch inside the airport lounge and then fly the rest of the way home the following morning.

And yet I continued to struggle with whether to stay there or continue my flight. *After all,* I reasoned, *it's only another 45-minutes.* The weather was clear with calm winds. *Why not make my first night flight? What could possibly go wrong?*

It was very tempting, but I had a nagging feeling that I shouldn't push it (it turned out to be a very good decision). With great reluctance, I picked a spot close to the terminal building and shut down the engine. I would later find out it was not the best place to park.

Stepping out of the airplane, I was engulfed by an eerie sense of silence. The cool air felt damp. There was no wind and no traffic. Not a single soul was around. Everything was just dark and still. It felt as if I had entered another dimension.

Most small airports have a combination lock on their buildings to prevent unauthorized people from entering after-hours. Only pilots have access to the combination because they know where to look for it. With this information, they can stop in anytime for a vending-machine snack or catch a quick nap before continuing to the next destination.

As I approached the small red brick building, I was surprised that the back door did not have a combination lock. I rifled through my mind, trying to remember if the airport facility directory had mentioned anything about it; I could have sworn it did. But upon closer inspection, I discovered that the backdoor was actually bolted from the inside!

"Drats! How am I going to get in? Where am I going to sleep tonight?" I said out loud.

Perhaps the front door has a combination lock, I thought.

I went around the building. No such luck.

Taking a deep breath, I surveyed my surroundings. The gravel parking lot was now illuminated by the moonlight, yet completely deserted. A single lane road alongside the airport was pitch black, overshadowed by towering pine trees on both sides. There was nothing for miles around.

Not ready to give up, I decided to try once more to get inside and made my way to the backdoor again. I rattled the doorknob aggressively, twisting, and pulling, but it wouldn't budge. Peering inside, I saw a faint outline of a couch. *How I wanted to get inside!*

Slowly turning around and leaning my back against the cold surface of the building, I stared at the silhouette of the airplane parked several feet away from me.

It was going to be a long night.

Making my way across the inky black ramp to the airplane, a gust of wind blew across the landscape, causing me to rub my arms vigorously. A fast-moving cold front was passing through.

Opening the door to the luggage compartment, I hurriedly sifted through my luggage, not remembering whether or not I had packed a sweatshirt. All I had was a remotely useful light-weight Gore-Tex jacket. In the far corner, I noticed something clumpy—thinking it was a blanket, my hopes surged, only to be deflated in one fell swoop when I realized it was a bunch of oily rags.

Feeling woefully inadequate for not being more prepared, I climbed into the cockpit, eased the door shut and felt the lock click into place with a resounding snap.

Sliding into the co-pilot's seat, I surveyed my makeshift hotel. A contortionist I was not—my expanding waist saw to that!

First, I attempted to stretch across the two front seats, curling into a fetal position, but when protruding seatbelt buckles poked at me menacingly, I tried lying on my back and then on my stomach. Nothing worked. This went on for hours. With each new position I tried, my legs were forcibly crammed into very unnatural positions.

Oh my.

That actually turned out to be the least of my problems. Not only was I shivering uncontrollably, but I'd made the mistake of parking right next to a powerful rotating beacon, the beams of which kept circling through the plane every 60 seconds. The way the white and green light flooded the cockpit reminded me of those prisoner-of-war movies where the rotating light from the guard post spills in and out of dark cells as it sweeps past.

An hour later, I finally fell asleep from sheer exhaustion. Why

I didn't move the plane to another spot, I'll never know!

At daybreak, I groggily looked outside the cockpit.

The entire airport was completely fogged in.

The fog swallowed up everything in sight, including the wings of the airplane. I knew I wouldn't be leaving anytime soon.

For three hours, I hungrily bumbled around the airport, finally open, waiting and watching the rising sun cut swaths of brightness through the fog. It was beginning to work its magic, because the surrounding tree lines, at first completely shrouded, were now becoming more visible with each passing minute.

Around 9 a.m. I decided I would wait another hour before taking the plane up for a "look-see" and circle directly above the airport to survey the surrounding area. If it was still foggy in the outlying areas, I would come right back down and wait some more.

At exactly 10 a.m., the "look-see" plan swung into action. I advanced the throttle wide open and the plane responded happily, jumping into the morning air with nary a bump. On the climb out, my head swung back and forth, scanning the land. Aside from an occasional wisp, the fog was mostly gone. Relieved, I punched my home airport identifier (KVLL, formerly known as 7D2) into the GPS and turned to the appropriate heading.

Within five minutes, my stomach was growling, reminding me that I hadn't eaten in a long time.

I'll be home in another forty-five minutes. You can wait.

It growled louder in defiance.

It was then I remembered that there was an airport along the way that had a restaurant on the field. I had been there several times before and the food wasn't too bad. Why not stop there?

But there was one problem: the airport had a control tower

on the field. How would I get in?

My mind did a quick flashback to the Kansas fly-in. One of the pilots had regaled me with his experiences with tower-controlled airports. All he had to do was contact the tower supervisor a day or two in advance to see if he could come in for a light gun landing on a specific runway.

A light gun looks like a big gun with red, white and green colored end pieces at the tip. It generates a powerful beam of light that can be seen even in the daytime. Light gun landings were used in the old days when there were no radios; they're used today in the event of a radio failure. A solid green beam from the tower means permission to land has been granted.

If the controller was willing to accommodate him, they'd set up an approximate time of arrival and select a runway. A special transponder code would be assigned so that the deaf pilot could be identified on radar when he was in the vicinity—usually three to five miles away from the airport.

As soon as the plane was seen on radar, the controller would seek him out via a pair of binoculars and upon spotting him, flash a powerful beam of green indicating he had permission to land immediately on the previously agreed selected runway.

As I recalled this conversation, I realized that I hadn't made any such arrangements with the tower controller. That's when I got creative. I smiled at the ingenuity of it.

Glancing at the Detroit aeronautical chart on my lap, I saw that the Jackson County Airport was encircled by broken blue lines with the number 35 enclosed in brackets. That meant that pilots could not enter their airspace between the ground up to and including 3500 feet without obtaining radio clearance.

"As long as I am at least 1,000 feet or more ABOVE that ceiling when I get there, I'll be fine," I said to myself.

I actually climbed to 5,500 feet, giving me a nice 2,000-foot buffer above Jackson's airspace. It would mean I'd have to descend almost 4,000 feet in a hurry once I got permission to land but I would worry about that later.

I entered the identifier of Jackson County Airport (KJAX) into the GPS and hit the "Direct To" button. It indicated that I would be there in about 20 minutes. The next thing was to get in touch with the air traffic controller and give him the surprise of a lifetime.

I announced, "Jackson Tower, this is a deaf pilot in Piper Archer 455H, 30 miles southwest. Will be requesting light gun landing for Runway 14."

I decided to let that sink in, hoping the controller understood me.

The red light on my radio stack immediately flickered to life. That meant someone was talking on this frequency. I was hoping the controller was not trying to call me back in confusion. If he was, maybe he didn't hear the part where I told him I was a deaf pilot.

Ten miles later, I had a Freudian slip of the tongue when I radioed him again.

"Jackson Tower, repeating that I'm a very hungry deaf pilot er, er, in Piper Archer 455H, now 20 miles southwest, er, er, will request light gun landing, er, er Runway 14."

My face felt hot but I pressed on, hoping for the best. At least I wasn't violating any rules. Five miles later, the large sprawling metropolitan airport came into view.

This time I had my radio act together: "Jackson Tower, deaf pilot in Piper Archer 455H, 15 miles southwest, will circle above airport at 5,500 for light gun signal, Runway 14."

After two more calls at the ten- and five-mile waypoints, I was finally on top of the airport. Banking the airplane 20 degrees to the left, I began to circle like a hawk, keeping an eye on the tower below me.

As I made my first round, I didn't see anything flash from the tower.

I double-checked the tower frequency: 120.7. It was the right one.

Puzzled, I made radio contact again: "Jackson Tower, deaf pilot, Piper Archer 455H, now circling above for light gun landing, Runway 14."

On the second trip around the bend, the tower still hadn't given me the green light. Something wasn't right. How long does it take to simply squeeze the light-gun trigger to give me permission to land on an otherwise quiet morning? There was hardly any traffic at that hour.

Entering the holding pattern a third time, I made the decision that if I was not granted permission to land on the third trip around the bend, I'd motor on home and try another time.

Just when I was about to finish the third and final circuit, I saw the brightest green beam of light from the tower. Beside myself with joy, I let out a rapid-fire response, "Jackson Tower, Piper Archer 455H. I see the green light, thank you. Will descend for left-base approach for Runway 14."

Since I was now cleared to land, I immediately began the 4,000-foot descent and headed southeast, away from the airport, so that I could enter the traffic pattern at the proper altitude.

After descending almost a thousand feet a minute and turning toward the airport, I made a respectable landing and got off the runway at the second exit. The tower immediately gave me a flashing green light, which meant I was given permission to taxi across another runway toward the ramp where I'd park the plane.

After parking, I climbed out and glanced up at the tower, shielding my eyes from the blinding sun. Someone from the tower was looking down at me. That must have been the guy who gave me permission to land. Feeling really proud of myself, I eagerly gave him two thumbs up.

I could barely see his face, but he appeared to be curling his finger back and forth. I couldn't tell if he was smiling or not. Suddenly feeling like a child guilty of committing a bad act, I pointed at myself, "Me??"

The faceless controller gestured to the bottom left to indicate where the entrance was.

Oh my God! Did I do something wrong? I thought.

Next to the door at the bottom of the tower was an intercom. Years earlier, I had learned a neat trick while living in New York City. Almost everyone had an intercom security system in their apartment buildings. I got in by pressing the doorbell and simultaneously pulling on the door handle until the person upstairs buzzed me in. I did it again that morning.

Closing the heavy vault-like door behind me, I saw before me a long, winding staircase that seemed to spiral upward forever. The steps were muddy and the walls murky brown, giving off a dark, ominous feel. I was immediately transported to an image of a castle from the Middle Ages. Taking a deep breath, I began the long ascent to the top.

I was met by a slender man slightly taller than me with a receding hairline. Clipped to the pocket of his polyester shirt was a government-issued badge with a badly outdated photo. He had looked a lot younger with gobs of hair back then. Glancing beneath the photo, I read, "Shift Supervisor." He was alone. The other controllers would probably be arriving soon.

Although uncertain and somewhat apprehensive at having

been summoned up to the tower, I tentatively offered my hand to thank him for the light gun landing.

To my surprise, he laughed heartily and said, "No problem at all. I was happy to help." In a split-second, the energy in the room instantly shifted from dark to light. Maybe I wasn't in trouble after all. But I still wasn't so sure.

It was then I noticed a huge red welt sprawled across his forehead. It looked fresh. Curious and concerned, I asked him about it.

"Sir, what happened to your forehead?"

With an air of self-deprecating humor, he said, "You know how it took me forever to give you the green light?"

"Oh yes!" I replied.

Pointing to a table in the corner, he continued, "Well, for the first time in my career, I had to crawl on top of that table to reach for the light gun that was attached to the ceiling. The problem was, I had trouble unlatching it, and when it finally came loose, it came crashing down on me!"

Suddenly feeling sorry for him, I stammered, "Jeez, I didn't mean to cause you so much trouble, sir!"

"Now, now, not a problem at all, Mr. Hopson. Enjoy your breakfast downstairs. When you are ready for takeoff, you will be using Runway 32 on the other side. Just radio us like you did this morning, and we'll take care of the rest."

Relieved that I really wasn't getting a verbal reprimand, I enthusiastically replied, "Well, thank you, Sir, I'll do just that!"

Bounding down the narrow staircase was a tad trickier than coming up. From this vantage point, the stairs seemed to spiral straight down into the abyss.

Reaching the ground level, I pushed the heavy door open and

stepped into the bright sunlight. Wiping the sweat from my forehead with the back of my hand, I made my way to the moderately busy restaurant next door. I picked a table by the window with a full view of the airport. I didn't recognize anyone there that morning.

A perky waitress quickly appeared out of thin air, magically extracted a pen from the back of her head, dabbed it on the tip her tongue and took my order. I decided to splurge and ordered a ham and cheese omelet with extra bacon, buttered whole-wheat toast and coffee. Quickly downing two cups of coffee and mopping the plate clean, I paid the waitress and went back out to the plane.

While conducting the pre-takeoff inspection, I kept glancing up at the tower, hoping to see my new-found friend looking out. I didn't see him. Perhaps he was busy tending to the morning traffic.

Once finished with the preflight inspection, I climbed into the aircraft and pressed the start button. Switching on the radios, I put in a call to the tower for permission to taxi. A flashing green light immediately came from the tower above me. Was it from the same controller? I couldn't tell.

Upon reaching the engine run-up area, I swung the plane around full-circle to face the tower so that I wouldn't have to crane my neck like Linda Blair in *The Exorcist*.

After the engine run-up check was satisfactory, I was ready.

"Jackson Tower, Piper 455H, request takeoff clearance, Runway 32." No need to tell them I was a deaf pilot. They already knew who I was.

A moment later, huge, gigantic blinds that covered the entire southeast side of the tower rose up majestically. It was like watching the curtains go up at a Broadway play.

Rather than giving me a solid green light like I expected, they gave me a flashing green light. That meant I was to taxi out to the runway and hold in position for further clearance. I felt like a Boeing 747 pilot taxiing into position with hundreds of passengers in the back, waiting for instructions to take off. It was an incredible feeling. Remember, this was the first time I was operating in an airport with a control tower!

The reason for the hold and release was soon apparent. A corporate jet was in the process of taking off from the adjacent runway. Watching the sleek jet climb 2,000 feet a minute held me transfixed. When the jet became a mere speck in the sky, I snapped back to reality and looked at the tower expectantly. The solid green beam of light would be coming soon.

A few seconds later it came. Excitedly thrusting the throttle wide open for maximum take-off power, the plane rose effortlessly into the pristine blue sky. At a thousand feet, I put her in a gentle climbing turn to the right and headed home. On my way up, I keyed the mike one last time to bid farewell to the controller. I imagined him smiling back at me. At his retirement party many years later, he would probably tell the story of a deaf pilot who once caused him bodily injury.

I would later learn that it was a good thing I hadn't attempted to fly home the night before. A pilot had had a gear-up landing accident (he forgot to put the landing gear down), causing my home airport to shut down for several hours.

Imagine the consequences had I not listened to my intuition and tried to make my first night flight back home! I would have been forced to divert to another airport, which, as a new pilot, could have made things even worse. There's no telling what I might have encountered on a night flight before I was ready.

Once again, I could only be grateful for the inner voice that guided me, balancing my adventurous spirit in the most perfect way.

Food for Thought: Have fun and be adventurous but be sure to act on your intuition, for it may save your life. Helen Keller once said, "Life is either a great adventure or nothing."

EXERCISE – CHAPTER TWENTY THREE

Like Helen Keller once said, "Life is a great adventure or nothing."

Let's take a look at some of the most adventurous aspects of your life. Did you end up doing something you normally wouldn't have but it turned out to be an incredible experience? What was that? How did it feel to go off the beaten path?

On the other hand, if you believe your life hasn't been adventurous enough, well, here's an opportunity to create one! What will you commit to doing in the next 30 days? Jot down what you've always dreamt of doing but haven't done yet. After doing that, make a firm decision that you will take inspired action when prompted by your higher self. Put your attention on it by visualizing yourself doing whatever it is you want to do. Creating a vision board and looking at it every day will help greatly. Then come back here and write about what happened at the end of 30 days.

TWENTY FOUR
THE NEVER-AGAIN FLYING EXPERIENCE

By the time winter of 2002 rolled around, the management at Oakland/Troy airport had undergone massive restructuring due to higher than expected operating expenses and let most of us, including me, go. But shortly after that, I found an opening for line service specialists at Berz Macomb airport.

My job was the same as before—towing planes, refueling them and providing customer service for pilots and their passengers. As an added bonus, Berz offered a very generous 50% aircraft rental discount for employees with a pilot's license. Of course, I took advantage of that program and flew as often as I could.

Rather than booking a commercial flight to fly to my parent's hometown (upstate New York) for the 2002 Christmas holidays, I decided to rent one of Bertz's small four-seat Piper Cherokees instead. This would be my second long distance flight, after the 555 mile trip I made to Kansas City.

In preparation for the 400-mile flight, I had two options. One was to fly south of Detroit, around the bend of Lake Erie, and east through the upper portions of Ohio and Pennsylvania before arriving in Schenectady, New York. The other was to fly straight through Canada, saving myself significant flight time as well as fuel.

Although it had been a year since 9/11, draconian airspace restrictions were still being heavily enforced around the nation. That meant if I wanted to fly through Canada, I was going to have to jump through regulatory hoops to make it happen. They had their own set of rules, further complicated by the fact that I wouldn't be able to maintain two-way radio communication through international airspace.

Since I absolutely, positively did not want to take the long way around Lake Erie, I enlisted the assistance of a very helpful air traffic controller to get me the required clearances ahead of time.

Apparently, this man had read about me in a magazine article published shortly after I had received my pilot's license the year before. He had sent me a congratulatory note, which I managed to find buried deep within my computer's email archives. Not only had he congratulated me on my aviation achievement but had also offered to help me in any way he could.

In response to my email, this controller jumped at the chance to make good on his word when I asked if he'd help make this flight possible. He lost no time making a flurry of phone calls to various control towers along the proposed route. And after weeks of effort on his part, I was eventually cleared to make my first international flight through Canada without the need to use the radio.

Winter that year (2002) was beset with howling blizzards, low-lying ice-laden clouds and poor visibility. My intention was to make it home in time for Christmas and, on Christmas Eve, after several nail-biting days, the weather finally turned for the better. I woke up that morning to a forecast of partly sunny skies and above-average visibility. Excited, I hurriedly packed my things and sped to Berz Macomb airport.

After pulling the plane out of the hangar and completing the required pre-flight check, a call was placed through a special telephone system to the faceless controller who had made all this possible. During the call, he gave me a unique four-digit code for the transponder device. Once the transponder was activated with this code, the airplane would appear on everybody's radar along the route, with a special note reminding them a deaf pilot was flying through their airspace.

It wasn't long before I was airborne, finally on my way home to upstate New York. The morning air was gloriously tranquil. It was 7:00 a.m. when I took off, and there I was, passing over homes full of sleeping occupants. The roads below barely had any traffic, for the town hadn't yet stirred. But I was bushy-eyed, full of excitement.

Since the airport I had just taken off from was on the east side of Michigan, it was only a matter of minutes before I crossed the Michigan-Canadian border. Despite the excellent weather (which gave me one less thing to worry about), my overactive imagination began painting a stark picture of international proportions.

What if one of the Canadian air traffic controllers experienced a technological glitch and could not identify me on radar? I might be seen as an unwanted intruder in their airspace, causing a flurry of fighter jets to be scrambled after me! You have to remember that the world was a little more paranoid after 9/11. Indeed, it was a very scary possibility, making me somewhat apprehensive for several minutes after penetrating the Canadian airspace.

Eventually, though, I succeeded in pushing those imaginary thoughts out of my mind and concentrated on the task of flying the airplane. There was not a lot to do once I leveled off. All I had to do was monitor the instruments, scan the airspace and keep the plane heading in the right direction.

No fighter jets are coming after me—everything is going to be okay.

Hit with renewed excitement, I shoved the throttle forward and began the long climb to 11,500 feet, putting me far above the scattered clouds. Despite the outside thermometer registering twenty below zero, I was nestled comfortably in my seat, fully enjoying the sun-drenched cockpit. The possibility of a Canadian fighter jet intercepting me along the way slipped further and further from my mind with each passing mile.

Another hour later, the portable GPS alerted me that I was fast approaching the Canadian-New York border, which meant it was time to begin the descent for landing to refuel. But when I looked down, I was shocked to discover that the innocent-looking puffy white clouds, once scattered, had transformed into a solid deck, completely obscuring my view of the land!

I had allowed myself to relax a bit too much, never noticing the gradual change taking place several thousand feet below me. At that moment it did not look like I could descend without putting myself through the clouds, which I was not yet trained to do.

My heart quickened.

I still had an hour and a half after crossing the Canadian-New York border before landing at Penn Yan Airport in the Finger Lakes region (New York State). Putting the plane in a gradual descent at a leisurely 500 feet a minute, I reached over to the passenger seat and rifled through weather data, hoping to find reports of clear skies in that area. The problem with weather reports is that the moment you print them, they're obsolete. That's how fast the weather can change, underscoring the importance of having a list of alternate airports to go to if the weather turned sour. I couldn't find what I was looking for, so I continued to motor on, hoping to see a break in the clouds up ahead.

When I was about 40 minutes away from Penn Yan airport, I finally saw what I was hoping for.

A very large opening.

Taking no chances, I immediately throttled back to idle and

put the plane in an emergency descend configuration. The plane dropped like a hot potato, literally diving at 2,000 feet a minute. When the airport finally came into view, the clouds above me slammed shut.

My heart was yammering like crazy. It was the first time I had ever had to use my emergency descent skills. But it wouldn't be the last time.

After landing, I put in a request for fuel and went inside the terminal to call my father (a special device for deaf people allows me to communicate with people by phone). To my surprise, he and my mother were already at the Schenectady County Airport waiting for me.

"But I won't be there for another hour and a half," I informed him.

"There is a surprise waiting for you here," he said. "Hurry up. After you get here, we still have a two-hour drive to your sister's house for dinner and we're already running behind schedule."

When I pressed him for details on the surprise, he was tight lipped.

Changing the subject, I asked, "Dad, what's the weather like over there?"

"It's gorgeous with clear, sunny skies. We're looking forward to seeing you soon!"

"Okay, I'll be there in a bit." And then I hung up.

One more call was made, this time to the air traffic controller at Schenectady County airport to let him know that I would be landing there within the next two hours. He was one of the long list of controllers who knew about my flight. This guy was expecting my phone call when it came in.

"You will be using Runway 28," he advised. Continuing, he

said, "When you get here, look for the green light gun signal from us. Your new transponder code for this leg of the flight is 4865. Don't forget to make your one-way radio call when you're about 10 miles out. Okay?"

"You got it!" I told him.

Back outside, I went through the pre-flight and hurriedly got back in the air, once again climbing to 11,500 feet. Between newly gathered weather reports obtained at the airport and Dad's weather observation in Schenectady, I figured I wouldn't have to worry about the clouds thickening up on me again.

The beauty of flying is that when you're a pilot, time flies very fast, especially if you're enjoying the flight, as I was on that day. Almost as soon as I leveled off at 11,500 feet, it was time to begin the descent again. In reality, an hour and a half had already gone by, but I hadn't even noticed it. As before, I put the plane in a gradual descent at 500 feet a minute.

But as I was going down, I was once again hit with the realization that the clouds had decided to play games with me and again formed a solid layer!

I couldn't believe it. It was happening all over again and not looking good.

This time there was the frightening possibility that I would have to abort the descent and wander around the sky looking for a hole to poke through. I hoped it would not come to that. Beads of sweat sprinkled across my forehead. It was a struggle to control the sickening feeling in the pit of my stomach.

Just what the hell had I gotten myself into?

Keying the mic, I put in a call to the tower, "Schenectady County tower, Piper Cherokee 56136 with deaf pilot on board, 10 miles west, landing Runway 28."

With only a few more miles to go, the cloud deck continued

to creep up to meet the underbelly of the airplane. At five miles from my final destination, the Piper Cherokee was barely skimming the tops of the clouds.

But as if the powers-to-be decided to give me a second chance, I was once again granted another glorious parting of the clouds, which formed a giant crater of a hole. My eyes feasted upon the delicious snow-covered landscape moving beneath me. The Schenectady County airport sprang into view; to my relief, the tower was already beaming me the green light.

Pulling the throttle back further, I gently pushed the nose down and entered the airport pattern. As I was doing that, the plane unexpectedly hit a pocket of mild turbulence and began bouncing around, causing my paperwork to fly around the cockpit. Apparently, the winds had picked up strength and were cascading up and down the hilly terrain. Despite the stiff crosswinds, I managed to make a safe, if not clumsy landing. Once landing and turning off to a taxiway, the tower sent me a flashing green light, giving me clearance to taxi over to the other side of the airport, where a line guy was positioned to direct me to my parking spot.

As soon as I shut down the engine, imagine my surprise when a bunch of reporters with TV cameramen in tow streamed out of the terminal and surrounded me. My immediate thought was that the controllers in Canada had alerted the authorities about an unidentified airplane flying through their airspace, setting off a terrorist scare. Dancing in my head were snappy headlines screaming, "DEAF PILOT VIOLATES INTERNATIONAL AIRSPACE!" Not a very pretty picture—but then I saw Mom and Dad calmly standing in the midst of all the chaos, smiling in unison.

I shot them a quizzical look, wondering what the commotion was all about. Several reporters were simultaneously hurling questions in my direction, probably forgetting that I couldn't hear them. What they all wanted to know was how a deaf pilot could fly unassisted for 400 miles without using the radio, especially through international airspace.

Seizing an opportunity to ham it up, I put on a great show. I remember thinking, *So this is what it feels like to be a celebrity. I love it!*

Unfortunately I was pressed for time because as my parents reminded me, we still had a two-hour drive ahead of us to my sister's house for dinner. With great reluctance, I cut the interviews short and left with my family.

On the way down, I learned that my folks had tipped off the press about this flight. Up to that point, they had made it clear that they didn't really believe I could become a pilot. This was their way of saying, "Sorry about that, but we're really, really proud of you and want the world to know about your achievements."

Tears sprang to my eyes in gratitude.

I further discovered that I had left Michigan at the right time on Christmas Eve because after I arrived home, nature proceeded to throw a hissy and dumped several feet of snow on Christmas Day. That was followed by a low pressure system that dominated the entire Northeastern seaboard, which meant had I decided to depart on the 25th, I would not have been able to open Christmas presents with my family. Ironically, this low pressure system meant I'd be stuck in New York for at least a few days before returning back to Michigan.

A courtesy call to the owner of Berz Macomb airport reassured me that they were not in a hurry to get their plane back. Apparently several years before, another renter pilot felt pressured to return the plane back on time but got caught in a major thunderstorm on the way and crashed. Not wanting to have another death on his conscience, the airport owner went out of his way to remind me not to mess with Mother Nature and to get back safely. Taking his message to heart, I spent three days waiting for the low pressure system to pass through.

On December 29, 2002, I finally got the break I was looking for. Dad and I piled into his truck at 8:30 a.m. and left for the Schenectady airport. Butterflies were churning like crazy in my stomach, which was normal, but mixed in there was a twinge of anxiety. There was 400 miles of flying to do in the middle of winter, where anything could happen!

Just as I pulled the plane out of the hangar, wet snowflakes began to fall.

Caught off guard, I pushed the plane back inside and borrowed several rags to wipe the plane down. I didn't like the idea of flying a wet airplane through subzero temperatures.

Meanwhile, the air traffic controller, the same one who had given me the light gun landing a few days earlier, came down from the tower to personally wish me well. When I voiced concerns about the unexpected snowfall, he informed me that it was a quick snow squall passing through, but that the sky behind it looked great according to his weather reports. He reassured me that I'd be okay. Checking the weather on the computer seemed to confirm this.

But the snow showed no signs of slowing down. Since the plane was dry as a bone by that point, all three of us—my dad, the controller and I, went inside the building next to the hangar and helped ourselves to coffee and hot chocolate. We hung around the lounge, chewing the fat until the sun finally broke through at one o'clock.

Due to the snowstorm, the airport was still buried under several feet of snow, but there were a couple of giant yellow plows spewing snow over to the side. Only Runway 28 over at the far side of the airport was clear. The other was halfway done, giving me just enough wiggle room to taxi over there for takeoff.

"Just follow my pick-up truck and I'll escort you over there," said the friendly controller. It must have been a strange sight for those outside the perimeter of the airport who just happened to witness a fiery red pickup truck driving down a half-plowed runway with a small plane following it. Too bad my father hadn't thought of bringing his camera—I would have loved to see what that looked like!

The engine check at the designated run-up area revealed no anomalies. The controller parked his truck several hundred feet ahead of me, off to the side. He was leaning against the hood, holding a hand-held radio and watching me. The plan was that after I was done with the engine run-up check, I'd give him thumbs up, at which point he would make a radio broadcast announcing my pending departure to the west.

Positioning myself on the runway, I waited for his hand signal for take off.

It came within seconds of sticking out my thumb. Slowly pushing the throttle forward, the plane gathered momentum and easily lifted into the sky, climbing 1,500 feet a minute. As I took off, I gently rocked the plane back and forth, bidding farewell to the controller. I saw him wave back. Dad was probably watching from the opposite end of the airport, but I couldn't see him. Still, I rocked the plane a second time, for his benefit.

On the way up, the clouds got closer. It was time to make a decision again. *Should I stay below or climb over them?*

Emboldened by the previous flight, I put the plane in a steep climb, zigzagging around the clouds to avoid touching them and was soon cruising at 10,500 feet. The cockpit was once again flooded with glorious sunshine.

Like before, once I leveled off, there was nothing to do but monitor the instruments, check fuel/oil pressure indicators, ensure the RPM was operating in the green and a host of other things. For a brief moment, my heart skipped a beat during the instrument scanning process when I noticed the fuel pressure gage bordering on red. But a slight adjustment of throttle and fuel mixture controls fixed the problem and the needle settled back into the green.

I was completely alone up there except when I spied a gorgeous blue and white corporate jet depositing long contrails in its wake several thousand feet below me. It sure gave literal meaning to the phrase "It's lonely at the top!"

Three hours after I had rocked the wings back in Schenectady, I began the descent for a fuel stop and a final weather update at a small airport in Akron, NY, just outside Buffalo. The New York-Canadian border was just fifteen minutes west of that airport.

On the way down, I saw what looked like a clearing just north of my flight path, but by the time I got there, it disappeared, forcing me to pull up. Although I could see the ground through patches of broken cloud layers, the holes were rapidly opening and closing like a fish's mouth. The small plane was simply not fast enough to poke through those fast changing holes.

My mind was racing, contemplating, strategizing, thinking and rationalizing.

How thick are the clouds?

How high is the bottom of the cloud level?

Should I do it?

NO, DON'T DO IT!

For several minutes I circled above, debating. The puffy, white clouds were busy transmuting themselves into all kinds of strange shapes and configurations. The wing tips were barely brushing by them.

Then I did something I never, ever thought I would do.

Cutting the throttle back to idle, I aggressively shoved the nose down and instantly disappeared into the clouds. The engine shook with rage while the plane slid down an invisible chute in total whiteout conditions, rendering me blind for a few seconds.

Less than a minute later, the plane sailed into the clear as if nothing had happened. Panting, I looked left and right to see if anyone else was around. No one was. But my eye caught a control tower in the distance behind me. In the mad dash through the clouds, I had inadvertently punctured the outer fringes of their airspace. That meant an irate controller in a bad mood with a pair of powerful binoculars could have easily read my plane's tail number, tracked me down and then reported me to the aviation authorities.

My heart raced at the thought. I found myself wishing the tiny airplane would magically transform itself into a mini-jet and race away as fast as possible.

As I moved farther to the west, I smacked my forehead hard, almost knocking myself unconscious when I realized had I flown another couple of miles above the clouds, I would have encountered clear blue skies and made a nice, uneventful descent.

At exactly 5:00 p.m., I landed at the Akron Airport and pulled up to the self-serve fuel pumps. Both tanks were quickly filled and paid for. A call to the weather briefer verified partly cloudy to clear skies with unrestricted visibility for the rest of the trip. Excited about completing the last leg of my flight, I lost no time getting back in the air. It was now 6:00 p.m. and the sun was starting to set. By this point, I had already accumulated almost a thousand hours of flight time and had plenty of night flying experience, so I wasn't worried about the sun setting this time.

As I was passing over the New York-Canadian border, Niagara Falls came into view, and I was instantly transported back to my childhood; my family had gone there for vacation a few times. Although it wasn't yet completely dark, the falls were already lit up in their brilliance. The sight made me smile.

Pulling on the yoke, I added full power and began to climb, but when I saw some clouds up ahead, I realized that it would not be a good idea to go above the clouds at night, because they're invisible and can turn deadly if you don't have an instrument rating. Turning around 180 degrees, I went right back down and went underneath them. It turned out to be the best decision I would make that night.

Comfortably settling at 4,500 feet, I watched with pleasure different cities light up the sky like Las Vegas. A well-lit bridge connecting the mainland to a small island off to the right added to the extravagant visual stimuli. Several large highways seemed to crisscross into a series of curves, loops and straight lines. The night air was extraordinarily calm, making for a super smooth flight. The plane was practically flying itself with very little input—I barely had to touch the yoke.

About halfway into the flight, the landscape began to alternate between large black spaces and tiny, remote villages with very few lights. But I wasn't worried. Everything was looking good and I would be home in just another hour or so. The Canadian-Michigan border wasn't far off.

Little did I know everything would come unglued in just a few moments.

The first warning sign came in the form of rainbow-like rings around streetlights down below. That should have alerted me that something wasn't right.

Then to my left, I noticed a faint outline of a runway, beckoning me to land there immediately. It was as if God put it there just for me. Unfortunately, I ignored it. That was the second sign.

Although the weather briefer had advised me to expect clear skies with unrestricted visibility, the city lights were gradually fading the closer I got to Michigan. At one point, I found myself squinting through the windshield without seeing much of anything. That was the third and final sign.

While subliminally trying to process all of this and wondering just what the heck was happening, BOOM, the airplane was suddenly swallowed whole in pitch blackness. It was as if I was in a black hole with absolutely no visual reference.

At once panic spread like wildfire, causing me to clench tightly on the yoke, over-controlling the airplane. It gyrated wildly, climbing, and then descending like a yo-yo a thousand feet a minute, temporarily rendering the plane out of control.

"I'M GOING TO DIE! I'M GOING TO DIE!" I screamed.

Fighting to regain control, I prayed fervently, using every available ounce of energy to concentrate on the panel-lit instruments. Somehow I managed to bring the airplane back under control and went lower so that I could see something on the ground—ANYTHING. Any pilot in his right mind would tell you that this was a disaster waiting to happen. Glancing at the altimeter, I was flying perilously low at 1,500 feet with very little forward visibility.

Suddenly a faint outline of a well-lit highway appeared through the murkiness. It crossed my mind to make an emergency landing there. Traffic was sparse and its width was larger than the runway I was planning to land on. But just as I was contemplating this course of action, a pair of red blinking lights mysteriously appeared a hundred or so feet above me.

And I was flying between them.

It took me a full minute to realize that they were among a cluster of cell phone towers in the area! There was no way I was going to land on the highway now that those cell towers were just within reach. I nervously flew a straight line between them.

Just as I thought things couldn't possibly get worse, I discovered the GPS was somehow incorrectly set up, taking me to the wrong airport! Instead of flying west, I was going northeast, taking me deeper into the murk.

Drawing every last bit of air I could fill my lungs with, I re-entered Berz Macomb Airport's identifier into the GPS with a very shaky hand. A new pink line was immediately redrawn on the screen of the GPS, and I gently turned several degrees to the left toward the correct heading. Fortunately, I was well past the towers by that point, but the deadly fog showed no signs of letting up. Completely relying on the GPS and the instruments, I honestly did not know whether I would survive the night. But I refused to give up.

With only three miles to go, the unimaginable happened.

God took one giant hand and literally wiped away the clouds in one clean swoop, instantly granting me unrestricted views of the entire metropolitan Detroit area! I thought I was dreaming. The spectacular sight was so overwhelmingly beautiful, I nearly missed Berz Macomb's faintly lit runway directly beneath me.

Wiping away tears of gratitude, I clicked the mic seven times to turn up the runway lights and made a perfect landing, a miracle considering both of my legs were shaking like a pair of jackhammers.

Slowly making my way over to the parking spot between the hangar and terminal building, I was surprised to see a small crowd quickly gathering on the brightly lit tarmac, because it was almost 10:00 p.m., when everyone should have gone home.

The moment I opened the cockpit door, five guys poked their heads in at the same time, their mouths agape. Their faces were begging for an explanation of what had just happened.

Someone handed me a cold bottle of water, lubricating my badly parched throat. My entire body shook like a washing machine while I took things out of the baggage compartment. As I was doing that, one of the guys leaned over to tell me that visibility was substantially less than a mile. Two of the guys were pilots themselves who were trying to get out but couldn't because of the weather. They were incredulous that I had made it in like that.

That's when I realized how dangerously close I had come to death that night. If it hadn't been for the handheld GPS, I might never have found Berz Macomb airport and simply wandered away into the abyss, meeting my maker that night.

I am not proud of the decisions I made that night. I understand the possibility of this story giving aviation, and deaf pilots in particular, an unwelcome black eye. But this was my experience, and I lived to tell the tale. That night, I learned a heap of lessons. I learned the importance of planning a flight more carefully. I learned not to take foolish chances like diving through the clouds. And I learned to land at the first available opportunity to wait for bad weather to change.

My arrogance morphed into humility. And it was the last time I ever took chances with flying.

Food for Thought: Overconfidence is just is bad as not having enough. Find a balance between the two and you'll be all right.

EXERCISE – CHAPTER TWENTY FOUR

Believe it or not, I was not one of those kids with a lot of confidence in the beginning. Even as a young adult, I was constantly working to bolster my inner strength. Having said that, when I became a pilot, something shifted. Suddenly I became confident – almost too confident, which is not a good trait to have in the cockpit. You saw what happened during the "Never Again" experience. My ego tricked me into continuing the flight when I should have made an unscheduled landing. When our ego gets in the way of seeing reality for what it is, that's when we get into trouble.

One example might be how you interpreted friendly advice from a close friend who was trying to point out an undesirable trait in you. Let's say you have an abrasive personality but no one has had the guts to tell you of this until one day a friend pulled you aside and brought it to your attention. Did your ego cause you to believe that you were being attacked and therefore you reacted defensively when in reality your friend was only trying to help you?

In other words, when have those "voices" from your ego prevented you from seeing reality clearly? What actions did you take as a result? How do you think you would have acted had you seen reality without your ego intervening?

TWENTY FIVE
LEEZA

Well, here we are, at the end of the book. In the beginning, I described how three words, uttered by Mrs. Jordan in her fifth grade classroom, caused a powerful ripple effect in a little deaf boy's life. Simply by shouting "THAT'S RIGHT, STEPHEN!" a seed was planted in my life, forever changing how I perceived my place on the planet.

Because Mrs. Jordan planted that seed in my young mind, I went on to experience a range of interesting situations, the highlights of which I have written about in this book.

Although the story I'm about to share with you is sequentially out of order, I felt it would be a great way to honor the power of those three words. You'll understand in a moment.

One day, I decided to take the power of gratitude up several notches. It was a Saturday morning. I was sitting on a black leather couch in my apartment in Manhattan (New York City), thinking about all the people in my life who had made a difference up to that point. While there were many, Mrs. Jordan's face swam into focus. The image of her powerful smile was crystal clear.

As soon as I saw her in my mind's eye, my attention immediately focused on finding a way to thank her. I got quiet and went within.

"Hey, why not thank her on a national talk show?" I mused.

The idea was powerful, but more importantly, it felt right. After firing off a letter to several national talk shows, I kept it a secret. Some ideas should be allowed to percolate and develop before they are made public. There's a time and place for everything, so I prayed that if it was meant to be, then the former teacher and I would be reunited at the right time at the right place.

Within two weeks, I heard back from *The View, Leeza* and *The Gayle King Show* (Oprah's best friend). From that moment on, everything was a dizzying blur.

Of the three shows, the producers of *Leeza* were quicker to make arrangements, while those at *The Gayle King Show* and ABC's *The View* both dragged their feet. My intuition told me to go with *Leeza* and not to wait for the others to make up their minds. I'm glad I did.

Mrs. Jordan was one of those teachers who never missed a day of class, so it was a challenge to convince her to fly out to California to "accept an award." Good heavens, her fifth grade students were far more important than some frivolous award!

She was so stubborn that the *Leeza* producers were forced to enlist the aid of her husband, her daughter, and even the school principal to convince her to appear on the show. Thanks to their Herculean efforts, they were finally able to cajole her into taking a few days off without revealing the real reasons for going.

Less than a week later, Mrs. Jordan and her daughter boarded a flight to Hollywood, while I took a different plane out of JFK, several hundred miles away.

When I arrived at the hotel, I was amused to learn that they were staying in a room directly above me! The taping wasn't scheduled until the next day. While I wanted to avoid the possibility of bumping into them, I didn't exactly relish the idea of being cooped up in the hotel and ordering room service. So I came up with a plan.

In the mood for a little local sightseeing, I put on a pair of dark sunglasses and my favorite baseball cap, and then I peeked out into the hallway before making a mad dash for the stairwell. Yes, I know, I've watched too many spy movies.

On the morning of the taping, hotel security came up to my room and escorted me to the service elevator for a ride down to the first floor, where a sleek black presidential-like limousine was waiting for me in the back of the hotel.

Forty-five minutes later, the unsuspecting fifth grade teacher and her daughter waltzed through the hotel lobby out to the front, where a bellhop was waiting at the door of another black limousine.

When my limo pulled through the security gates at Paramount Pictures and dropped me off at the *Leeza* studios, I was immediately escorted to the "green room," where guests enjoyed an assortment of tea, coffee and pastries before going on the air. I was grateful they had a bottle of cold water available—my mouth was parched.

Taking small sips of ice cold water, I was looking around the room at the various photos of previous guests when a sudden opening of the door startled me. A frazzled-looking woman with curly hair identified herself as one of the producers. She held out a tape recorder and breathlessly told me to make a quick recording of what I wanted the teacher to hear before we were reunited. I said something along the lines of "Mrs. Jordan, you made a very big difference in my life many years ago, and I am here to thank you for it." The producer snatched the tape recorder from me and disappeared. I was alone again.

Not more than five minutes after she had left, she was back. Poking her head inside the room she mouthed the words, "Okay, it's time now. Please follow me." A rush of excitement coursed through my body. *Here we go.* The producer efficiently led me to a chair in the studio, where Leeza and the audience were waiting.

Stepping into the glare of hot lights and in front of several large cameras threw me for a loop. Every single eye was following me to my assigned seat. Leeza was sitting with the audience with a heavy mailbag on her lap. I nervously whispered into the ear of one of the assistant producers to request another glass of water.

Without warning, the cameras began to blink and the taping began. Fortunately Leeza was very easy to lip-read even at a distance so I calmed down considerably, knowing everything would be okay.

Eventually she made her way down the steps, alternating her focus between the cameras, the audience and me. Easing herself into the chair next to me, Leeza started by asking me what it was that Mrs. Jordan had done for me over thirty years ago. Then she had me read the letter I had written to the show, after which I told the audience how the announcement of those three words, "THAT'S RIGHT, STEPHEN," forever changed my life. That was followed by questions from Leeza about my background.

When she was finished, she pointed to the double doors to the right of where I was sitting, and said, "Stephen why don't you step over to the other side and hide behind those doors? When it's time for you to come out and surprise Mrs. Jordan, one of the technicians will signal you."

On my way to the hiding place, I stretched out my arms in the air and said with a grin, "I hope she recognizes me!"

Leeza then called out to the teacher, who had been safely tucked away in a sound proof room the entire time I was on camera, "Okay, come on out, Mrs. Jordan."

A large camera on rollers was positioned by the entrance to the studio so that viewers could watch the apprehensive teacher make her way onto the stage. Leeza guided Mrs. Jordan to her seat and gave her a couple seconds to get comfortable.

"Do you know why you're here today, Mrs. Jordan?" Leeza inquired.

"No," she replied apprehensively.

"Well, it's a good thing. *It's a very good thing.* Someone wrote to us and said that you are to be honored for making a very big difference in this person's life. We're going to play a tape to see if you recognize this person's voice."

"Okay," she said, now quivering. She went to pull out a Kleenex, almost knocking the box off the table.

While this was going on, I was watching everything through a closed-circuit monitor on the floor. When she first walked in, I almost let out a gasp because she looked exactly the same and not a day older! I couldn't believe my eyes.

Leeza nodded to some invisible technician to play the recording.

The main camera zoomed in closer to Mrs. Jordan. As the tape played, an instant flash of recognition spread across her face, causing tears to well up.

"Mrs. Jordan, do you know who that was?" Leeza asked gently.

"Yes."

"Well, who was it?"

Stifling a sniffle, she said, *"Stephen Hopson."*

My hand flew to my mouth.

Leeza nodded to the invisible technician, who suddenly materialized next to me. It was time to go out and greet my former teacher for the first time in over 30 years.

Shoving the fragile stage door wide open, I slammed my right foot on the floor the same way she had over 30 years ago and extended my arms, inviting her to come and hug me.

The teacher made her way to where I was standing and hugged me tightly. Putting my left arm around her, I made a sweeping motion with my right hand over the audience and whispered, *"All of this is for you."*

We made our way back to our seats and she pulled out another Kleenex, this time knocking the box to the floor.

"Oops."

"Mrs. Jordan, you remember Stephen extremely well?" Leeza asked.

Dabbing her eyes, she nodded.

"What do you remember about Stephen?" Pictures of me as a fifth grader flashed on the screen behind us.

Glancing upward to gather her thoughts, Mrs. Jordan said, "Well, he was enthusiastic and a hard worker."

Leeza turned to me and said, "Stephen, would you like to say a few words to her?"

Grabbing the former teacher's hand, I positioned myself so that we were looking directly at each other in the eye, and said, "Mrs. Jordan, you made a very big difference in my life over 30 years ago. You took me under your wing and believed in me. You said "THAT'S RIGHT, STEPHEN" which forever changed my life. You're here on the show today because I wanted to thank you for that."

She reached for the Kleenex box again, with Leeza standing nearby—just in case. Literally sobbing, Mrs. Jordan said, "Thank you Stephen, *thank you.*"

No, no, Mrs. Jordan, thank YOU for having confidence in me.

Food for Thought: When you practice the power of gratitude in a big way to someone who's made a difference in your life, you can bet that it will generate a life-changing ripple effect in that person's life.

EXERCISE – CHAPTER TWENTY FIVE

What was the biggest thing you did to express your heartfelt gratitude toward someone?

On the other hand, self love and appreciation is just as important as to what we do for others. Have you done anything recently to express gratitude toward yourself? For example, I remember years ago there was this particular brand of cologne that I really liked but it was priced higher than I was willing to pay for. Then one day I realized that I was just as deserving of having that bottle of cologne as anyone else and decided to splurge. WOW, what a great feeling it was to have given myself such a nice treat! What about you? Have you always wanted to spend a day at the local spa? Well, what's stopping you?

Commit to doing 3 things this week to appreciate yourself and 3 things to show appreciation to someone else.

AFTERWORD: A NOTE FOR PARENTS OF DEAF CHILDREN

Parents of deaf children who are sometimes part of the audience at my speaking engagements often approach me afterwards, their worried eyes full of questions. They're not hard to spot. Seeing that I am successful and articulate, they almost always want to know whether their hearing impaired child (or children) should be mainstreamed and taught how to speak right from the get-go or learn how to sign.

My folks were adamant that I not learn sign language as a child; they didn't want me to become dependent on something that the vast majority of the world did not use. If they had made that decision today, the Deaf Community would probably be in an uproar over it; the prevailing belief now is that sign language should be taught at the earliest possible age.

It always breaks my heart to see them struggle over this monumental life-altering decision. I always give the same answer to this question. While mainstreaming and adopting sign language much later in life (in college) worked very well for me, it may not necessarily work as well for others, because everyone is different. I remind them to listen to their own intuition, coupled with faith and prayer.

ABOUT THE AUTHOR

The author in many ways has been preparing all his life to write this book. Despite being deaf since birth, Stephen J. Hopson enjoyed fifteen years of extraordinary success in the turbulent world of Wall Street before switching gears in 1996 and becoming a transformational speaker, author and eventually pilot. During the last five years he was on Wall Street, Stephen enjoyed a lucrative career as a stockbroker with numerous sales and recognition awards at financial giant Merrill Lynch.

Stephen is a risk-taker with a capital "R." After several years of smashing barriers on Wall Street, he experienced an epiphany in April 1996 that inspired him to "chuck it all" and leave a lucrative 6-figure career and take a leap of faith into uncharted waters. Family, friends and colleagues were flabbergasted. They couldn't understand why he would leave a good career where he was making a lot of money, winning awards and being profiled extensively in the national media, including *The New York Times, Careers and the disabled* (cover story) and *CNN*. At the time, it had been a while since he last had a public speaking engagement and he did not have any writing credentials to speak of. What's more, he had no proof that taking such a huge a leap of faith and starting a new career would actually pan out. It was as if he was riding on some kind of jet stream propelling him forward to live his life's purpose. He just knew it would all work out.

Today, he is in demand nationwide as a transformational speaker and is contributing author to three books, including the best-selling *Chicken Soup for the College Soul* (Health Communications, Inc., July 1999), *heartwarmers* (Adams Media Corp., March 2000) and *MAGICAL SOUVENIRS: True Mystical Travel Stories From Around the Globe* (Hay House, June 2001). He has appeared on several talk and radio shows including *Leeza* and *The Mitch Albom Radio Show*. His story has been featured in numerous newspapers and magazines around the world.

Stephen Hopson never dreamt that leaving Wall Street would ultimately lead him to the rapid fulfillment of his largest childhood dream, which was to become a pilot. A few years after he left Merrill Lynch, he stumbled onto a website about deaf pilots. His long-buried dream immediately came roaring back to life, and he began flight training in 2000. After many months of training, he finally earned his private and commercial pilot's licenses (2001 and 2003 respectively).

But that was not all.

In February 2006, he made aviation history by becoming the world's first deaf pilot to earn an instrument rating, which actually requires the use of a radio when flying though inclement weather. Through Stephen's unwavering faith, courage and hope, the FAA (Federal Aviation Administration) was finally convinced that he could be pilot-in-command of an aircraft through the clouds with the help of a qualified co-pilot handling the radios for him. This was an unprecedented accomplishment, since no deaf pilot had ever achieved such a rating in the history of aviation. It was an achievement that garnered worldwide media attention from places as far away as France, Ireland, Korea, Australia and Sweden.

About three years after his aviation achievements, he decided it was time to go back to school but not just any old school. What he wanted was something different, something deeper than what traditional schools offered. Not knowing where to begin, he did a Google search using the words "spiritual psychology." The result of that search led him to Maharishi University of Management (MUM) in a small, magical town called Fairfield, Iowa. Almost immediately he knew he found the right school and was matriculated for the 2009-2010 Vedic Science graduate program. That's when he discovered the existence of Transcendental Meditation® (TM). He credits TM for helping him reconnect to the inner reservoir of creative intelligence, the source of all that there is. After several months of TM, he decided he wanted to accelerate his spiritual growth and applied for and was accepted into the TM-Sidhi program, thereby becoming the first deaf person to do so. The purpose of the TM-Sidhi program is to accelerate the benefits gained from the TM technique by training the mind to think from the level of what is called Transcendental Consciousness, the mind's source. He credits TM-Sidhi for taking his professional speaking and writing career to even greater heights.

As a transformational speaker, Stephen's explosively powerful keynote speeches encompass the fundamental success and spiritual principles that govern and shape his life. Stephen's gift is that he speaks from his heart, sharing poignant, yet humorous stories of a man who lives his life as a spiritually alive person connecting with others in the human experience, holding audiences spellbound. Passionately taking his audiences on a spirited journey of self-discovery, Stephen shows how the principles he lives by can positively influence their thinking, actions, values and lives. He offers the insights necessary for individuals to transform themselves into the loving spiritual and human beings they ultimately want to become.

Audiences have said that when they heard him speak, their hearts opened, their minds were inspired and their bodies were moved into positive, life-transforming action because after hearing his story, they cannot possibly go back to "life as usual" and continue to make excuses for themselves.

To book Stephen for a speaking engagement, please contact him at **www.sjhopson.com**

OBSTACLE ILLUSIONS

LaVergne, TN USA
24 March 2011
221470LV00001B/4/P